Bouncing Back

Bouncing Back

107 Tips To Become More Resilient

Hyacinth Fraser and Eva Provedel

First published in the UK in 2020

ISBN 978-1-5272-6251-5

To family and friends who have supported us during this time and throughout our lives.

Contents

Preface

This book came to life during the early stages of the Covid-19 pandemic as a response to the challenges that are affecting us and will affect us in the future.

Now more than ever we need to tap into our resilience and resources, not only to learn from hardships, but also to come out stronger, wiser and more equipped.

We devised 107 practical tools and techniques to become more resilient, now and in any situation where we might struggle.

These are tools for *you* – reader – to try out and practice. The numbers don't indicate a particular order. You can choose to follow the order or jump between chapters – see what attracts you and what you feel like experiencing.

We believe that through practice and action, you can change your perspective and behaviours for the better, and by changing these, you will have an impact on the outside world. You can have more control.

But don't forget kindness and self-compassion – these will also prove crucial along your journey.

We hope you'll be inspired to action, and wish you a bright future ahead.

Eva and Hyacinth, 2020

Introduction and how to use this book

Thank you for joining us on this journey of resilience. It feels like it's an everyday commitment to stay positively focused. It is not a 'one and done': it is a continuous process.

Resilience can be considered a decision. Even where there is a pull to do otherwise, each and every day we can make a choice to get up and pull/push through those difficult moments.

You will find 107 chapters with our tips for resilience, divided into 9 sections. The sections are:

Appreciation & Celebration
Self-Reflection & Awareness
Taking Charge, Taking Action
Support & Community
Mindfulness & Listening
Goals & Mindset
Wellness & Self-Care
Learning and Motivation
Reframing & Visualising

Each chapter offers an inspiring quote followed by our insights, an activity and two resources: a book and a video (with video-links up and running at the time of publishing). The activities offer practical tools and techniques that are at the heart of the experience. We encourage you to take action.

How to use this book – there are any number of ways:

You may decide to read it from beginning to end as though you were reading a novel and then go back in and dip into your favourite part of the book to undertake the activities.

You may choose to start at the beginning and go through each of the activities by chapter in turn, or you may choose to open the book randomly and decide to read that page and undertake the activity.

You may also choose to explore a particular section at a time, based on what you are drawn to, and we invite you to revisit the chapters you resonate with after some time, to find out if there are new insights there for you.

There is no right or wrong way, it is your choice. We believe there is something in this book for everyone, no matter what part of your resilience journey you are on.

We hope you enjoy the book and we would welcome your feedback in terms of how the book has helped you and what else you would like to see in an updated version.

Definitions of Resilience

The capacity to recover quickly from difficulties.

(Lexico, powered by Oxford Dictionary)

The ability of a substance to return to its usual shape after being bent, stretched or pressed.

The ability to be happy, successful again after something difficult or bad has happened.

(Cambridge Dictionary)

In physics, resilience is the ability of an elastic material (such as rubber or animal tissue) to absorb energy (such as from a blow) and release that energy as it springs back to its original shape. The recovery that occurs in this phenomenon can be viewed as analogous to a person's ability to bounce back after a jarring setback. Author Pelham Grenville Wodehouse referred to resilience as "a sturdy refusal to acknowledge defeat."

The word Resilience derives from the Latin verb re-salire, meaning "to jump back" or "to recoil."

(Merriam Webster)

Appreciation & Celebration

1. Celebrate your successes

"Our resilience increases as we recognize the magnitude of what we have already accomplished." Patricia O'Gorman

Recognising and acknowledging your successes is a very effective confidence booster. It is often easy to focus only on what has gone wrong and beat ourselves up for it. Instead, wouldn't you want to be fair with yourself, in the same way you would with a good friend?

Looking back at your successes also gives you the tools to analyse what skills and resources you put into place in that situation. It is a great tool for personal belief and empowerment.

Activity

a. Divide a page into 3 columns.

b. In the first column, make a list of 15 achievements in the last 3 months – things you did that you are proud of and went well. For example, you completed a report on time.

b. In the second column, add more details on what you did specifically that assisted the successful outcome. For example, you set milestones for yourself during the process and were able to focus completely on the task without interruptions.

c. In the third column, extract and write down the skills you have demonstrated in the completion of each achievement. For example, you demonstrated time management skills and mindfulness on the task.

d. Looking back, what do you notice? Are there any revelations? Note them down at the end of the page.

Resources

Hibbert, Noor – Just F*cking Do It: Stop Playing Small. Transform Your Life.

Burchard, Brendon – Celebrate the Small Wins

2. Write a list of things that make your heart sing

"Being the richest man in the cemetery doesn't matter to me. Going to bed at night saying, I've done something wonderful. That's what matters." Steve Jobs

This will be different for each of us. Some of the items I would include on my list is poetry, favourite authors, wonderful books, music - I have a pretty eclectic taste from classical to reggae and a combination of the two, landscapes, podcasts etc. As I am writing this, I'm feeling more and more energised. This list helps me to know that at any point I need an injection of encouragement, I can hop over to my list and get it.

This list you're creating for yourself will help you to push through, to go around, to go under, to go over any potential difficulty. It's not always possible to arrive at what you might perceive as an absolute perfect solution; it will though enable you to arrive at a perfect solution for that moment in time. Trust yourself.

Activity

a. Create at least four headings: for me it might be – music, books, holidays, podcasts.

b. Under each of these headings write at least seven items that make your heart sing, for example, under books, I would write seven of my favourite books or seven books I look forward to reading

c. Programme some of these activities into your diary

Resources

Singer, Michael A – The Untethered Soul: The Journey Beyond Yourself

Motivation Hub – Living Your Dreams – Motivational Video Compilation

3. Remind yourself that you are worthy

"When we learn how to become resilient, we learn how to embrace the beautifully broad spectrum of the human experience." Jaeda Dewalt

Have you heard of the Inner Critic? The inner critic is a voice of criticism that most people experience in their heads. Most people have it, and find it hard to balance it with their inner Coach, a supportive voice.

The good news is that you are in charge of your thoughts. Reminding yourself of your worth will go a long way to build your self-confidence, and when you believe in yourself, you will shine brightly for others too.

Activity

a. Write down 10 things you appreciate about yourself – explore the physical, mental and spiritual elements of yourself. Get specific about exactly what you appreciate and why.

b. On a separate piece of paper, note the last 5 pieces of positive feedback you received from people you trust. If they are vague, go back to those people and ask them what exactly they appreciated you doing or saying.

c. Now choose one way to treat yourself today and each day for the rest of the month. This could range from forms of self-care (that bubble bath you haven't had in a while) to doing things for yourself that you have been putting off. Write one thing on each day of the month on your calendar... and enjoy!

Resources

Peters, Steve – The Chimp Paradox: The Acclaimed Mind Management Programme to Help You Achieve Success, Confidence and Happiness

Brown, Casey – Know your worth, and then ask for it

4. Be kind to yourself

Forgive yourself for your faults and your mistakes and move on." Les Brown

If your friend or colleague came to you upset and told you about an issue they are struggling with, what would you do? Perhaps you might offer them a glass of water, sit down with them and listen.

What would you say to them? Perhaps you might offer words of encouragement, empathy, support. What would you do for them? Perhaps there is something you could offer to help with, or ask them how you might be supportive for them.

Do you typically treat yourself with the same level of support, empathy and kindness as you would with those friends? Often times the answer is no. We are way harsher with ourselves, and our inner critic has many ways to beat us up, even when things are going well.

Activity

a. When something goes well, congratulate yourself and decide how you will celebrate your success or milestone. Think about something that you did well today, or this week. Choose a self-reward and plan it in your diary now.

b. When things are not going so well, instead of succumbing to self-criticism and self-bashing, what might you say to yourself in the same way you would speak kindly to a friend?

c. Finally, with kindness and empathy, recognise what areas you might need to improve on, and make a plan for it. If you think you need to improve your ability to give feedback, for example, think of all the different ways in which you can learn more about it and when you can practice it.

Resources

King, Vex – Good Vibes, Good Life: How Self-Love Is the Key to Unlocking Your Greatness

Markovic, Jelena – The power of self-kindness

5. Write three things that you are grateful for

"You cannot do a kindness too soon because you never know how soon it will be too late." Ralph Waldo Emerson

Being grateful helps us to stay resilient and positively focused as well as generate life-enhancing emotions such as joy and happiness. Gratitude helps us to be responsive rather than reactive with our emotions. It means we can generate more control over what we think and feel.

Gratitude helps us deepen who we are at our core. It leads to deeper relationships. We can make better choices around our goal achievements. Focusing on what we are grateful for could lead to better health through increased depth of sleep and more energy when we need it.

Activity

a. Write three things that you are grateful for at least twice a day, last thing at night and first thing in the morning.

b. At the end of each week have a look over your gratitude's and write a paragraph about how these gratitude's make you feel.

Resources

Good Days Start With Gratitude: A 52 Week Guide To Cultivate An Attitude Of Gratitude: Gratitude Journal

Motiversity – Gratitude - Best Motivational Video Speeches Compilation - Listen Every Day! Morning motivation

6. Congratulate yourself

"You never let a serious crisis go to waste. And what I mean by that it's an opportunity to do things you think you could not do before." Rahm Emanuel

All too often we give ourselves a hard time about what we could have done more of, what we could have done less of, what we didn't do well, that we are not good enough, etc. and the list goes on.

Time to take a chill pill and notice what you do well and give yourself a pat on the back.

Activity

Take 15 minutes just to yourself and think about the last 7 days. Note all the things you have done well, including things people have told you that you have done well.

Resources

Samit, Jay – Disrupt Yourself

Samit, Jay – It's Time To Disrupt You

7. Remind yourself of all the reasons why you are skilled and competent

"No one can make you feel inferior without your consent." Eleanor Roosevelt

A lot of people suffer from the imposter syndrome: an imminent feeling that they will be soon found out. It is a feeling that they are not *really supposed* to be there, or that they *don't really know* what they're doing, even if they've done it for many years. Sound familiar? Many people experience this in the work context, though not exclusively, there may be situations outside of work where this plays out too.

Remember, there is a good reason you were selected for your job and people look to you for advice on certain things. The time has come to stop waiting for external validation, and to acknowledge your competence for yourself.

Activity

a. Write down a list of skills you know you are good at, for example: are you good at supporting people? Are you organised? Perhaps you're great at problem-solving. You can write "being" titles, such as: honest, professional, supportive, etc.

b. Once you have the skills, add a note about what these words mean to you. If you wrote 'professional', for example, describe what that means to you in terms of behaviours: does it mean delivering work on time or perhaps remaining calm under pressure, or both and more? Write all your notes besides or under each skill. This will help you identify the many different ways in which each skill is displayed. Make sure what you write here is the "doing" bit, the behaviours: these usually start with an active verb, which has "I" as a subject (i.e. I delivered the work on time; I set milestones; I took breaks, etc.). Suggestion: use bullet points.

c. Once you have your behaviours, add a note besides each behaviour to remind yourself of specific situations in which you displayed it. Be very specific: which projects did you deliver on time recently? When and in which situations did you stay calm in the face of pressure? Add both work and out-of-work situations. Add as many as you can think of.

d. Look back at your list. How does it make you feel?

e. If you start doubting yourself, take a deep breath and think about why you are the right person for the job. Remind yourself of the other times you 'handled it' and how this enabled you to address the new situation effectively. Take a look at your list: it will bring those situations to mind quickly.

f. Keep building your skills-list. This will be useful in the future for job-related conversations and, more importantly, to boost your confidence.

Resources

Cope, Andy, & Whittaker, Andy – The Art of Being Brilliant

Duckworth, Angela Lee – Grit: the power of passion and perseverance

8. Forgive yourself

"Forgive yourself for not knowing what you didn't know before you learned it." Maya Angelou

No one is perfect. Where you need to forgive yourself – do so. It doesn't help to hold on to historical baggage. Let it go and notice how much lighter you feel.

Activity

Write yourself a letter of self-forgiveness.

Resources

Vanzant, Iyana – Forgiveness: 21 Days To Forgive Everyone For Everything

Winfrey, Oprah – Oprah's Forgiveness Aha Moment

9. Write down what you appreciate about yourself

"Resilience is knowing that you are the only one that has the power and the responsibility to pick yourself up." Mary Holloway

Most people find it easier to appreciate others than themselves, however, if you are not the one to see your own qualities and skills, how can you expect others to fully see them?

Putting any potential humility and embarrassment aside, this is a chance for you to really see and acknowledge to yourself and for yourself what you appreciate about you.

Activity

a. Pick a journal and a pen, and find a quiet space to sit and write for 10-15 minutes.

b. Write down the qualities you appreciate about yourself. Start the sentence with "I appreciate that I am…." (for example: kind, determined, loyal, supportive, strong…etc).

c. By each quality, add one or more examples of when you exhibited it. For example, when was the last time you were supportive? Who with? What did you do that highlighted that quality? Having examples in your head to "back it up" will give you even more confidence in your qualities.

d. You can use this for work too. If you are looking for a promotion or another job, think about the qualities you have that would fit that job, and make a list of the examples when you exhibited those traits. Pick some examples that are relevant to the role you are applying for.

Resources

Wallace, Stuart – The Power Of Self-Talk: How To Stop Beating Yourself Up, Take Action And Achieve Success In Your Life

Saligari, Mandy – Feelings: Handle them before they handle you

10. Write a love letter to yourself

"Self-love is not so vile a sin as self-neglecting." *Shakespeare*

We live in a world where it sometimes gets difficult to focus on yourself. To really celebrate your triumphs. A focus on self is really important. If we don't, how do we get to focus on others? We need to put fuel in our tank to make sure we can continue on in an empowered way. There are people that rely on you and you can't give to anyone, unless and until you give to yourself.

So, what does this mean? It means recognising that you are good enough. Recognising that you are worthy of love, including self-love.

Activity

a. In your love letter to yourself, complete the following questions:

I. The top three things I appreciate about myself are….

II. The top four things I would like to achieve for myself over the coming year are…

III. The top five action steps I am going to take to ensure my achievements in the coming year are...

IV. Write six affirmations (The definition of affirmation is the act of confirming something to be true, or is a written or oral statement that confirms something is true. An example of affirmation is reminding yourself how smart you are - "I am smart and always have been"), you can use these affirmations to turn up the volume to support your love of self.

V. Say your affirmations to yourself every day, at least once a day.

b. Journal your year ahead and notice the changes that are taking place in you and for you.

Resources

Cotton, Fearne – Quiet: Silencing The Brain Chatter And Believing That You Are Good Enough

Lavendaire, Aileen – Self Love Journaling Prompts

Self-Reflection & Awareness

11. Write down three things you need

"Your vision will become clear only when you can look into your own heart. Who looks outside, dreams; who looks inside, awakes." Carl Jung

It is so easy to go about life forgetting to check in with ourselves. Our body has a way of letting us know when things are starting to become intolerable.

Listening to yourself is paramount to being self-aware. This starts with being aware of your needs, of whichever nature they are. Maybe you need to take a break, or you need to talk to someone, or you need some sunshine. This is a practice of listening to your needs.

Activity

a. Stop what you are doing, close your eyes and take a few deep breaths.

b. Check in with yourself: what do you need right now? Write down 3 things.

c. Widen the scope: what do you need this week? Note down 3 things.

d. This month? 3 things.

e. This year? 3 things.

f. What do you need in this job / relationship / role or you-name-it? 3 things.

g. What have you noticed? … 3 things!

Resources

Meurisse, Thibaut – Master Your Motivation: A Practical Guide to Unstick Yourself, Build Momentum and Sustain Long-Term Motivation

Lefebvre, Mathias – What do we truly need in our lives?

12. Ask questions of the situation

"Take all the courses in your curriculum. Do the research. Ask questions. Find someone doing what you are interested in! Be curious!" Katherine Johnson

Some great questions to ask include: what is at issue here? How can I think about this differently? What are the hindering factors? What are the helping factors? What are the background issues I need to consider? Who or what can help? What is the end goal? What has led up to things as they currently are? What can be learned from this situation for the future?

Activity

a. Ask yourself some great questions.

b. Implement the answers as appropriate.

Resources

Robbins, Anthony – Awaken The Giant Within

Vaughan, Mike – How To Ask Better Questions

13. Journal about an issue

"The human capacity for burden is like bamboo- far more flexible than you'd ever believe at first glance." Jodi Picoult

Some issues are really hard to crack. Have you ever found yourself obsessing over a problem or a situation and becoming more and more frustrated about it? The first thing you can do is take a break from it: step away for a while – go for a walk or do something else – and then come back to it.

When you come back from your break, you could try some journaling about it. It helps to uncover your feelings around it and then logically break it down and see what solutions come up. You don't even have to aim for a particular solution: you can simply write *about* the issue in free-flow, let it all out, and allow yourself to be surprised by the outcome. Writing will help you process the problem and it often is described as a cathartic way to cope with it.

Activity

a. Find a spot to write. Set yourself up with a notebook, something to drink and a timer. Make sure you have at least 30 minutes free of distractions and interruptions.

b. Start writing about the context of the issue itself: how it arose, who is involved, what the history is. How would you describe it to someone who has never heard about it?

c. Now explore your feelings around it. Are you frustrated, angry, sad? Where do those feelings come from? What is a coping mechanism that could work for you to manage your feelings so that they don't cloud your judgment? All feelings are valid and you can put them down on paper so that you can move your focus onto a solution-based approach.

d. Now break down the issue into its different parts. Explore your wants and needs in this situation. Explore the outcome you want.

e. If the issue involves any type of conflict or different points of view, imagine you're the other party involved, and describe it from their point of view? What do they want or need? How do they feel about it? Imagine you are them; you are wearing their shoes. You can repeat this with any number of parties, and gain insight on their point of view.

f. Now imagine you are a third entity in the picture and you're seeing the issue and all the parties from above. How would you describe the dynamics between the people involved? Where do you see the issue from here, and what would you suggest to the parties, so that they are able to move towards a resolution?

g. Having gathered more insight on the situation and different points of view, how might you help things move towards a positive outcome, keeping in mind your needs and other parties' needs too? Write everything that comes to mind.

h. Once you stop writing, check in with yourself: how are you feeling now? What new perspectives have you gained on the problem?

Resources

Rasheta, Noah – The 5-Minute Mindfulness Journal: Daily Practices for a Calmer, Happier You

Kirby, Andrew – What I Learned by Journaling for 730 Days

14. Align your work and life to your values

"Your goals and the tasks you choose to accomplish your goals either align with your dream and core values or they don't. It's that simple." Julie Connor

Values are so important yet so unspoken about. They represent what is universally important to you and literally drives your behaviour, whether you are aware of it or not. Sometimes you might not know why you're feeling frustrated or angry, and it might well be that someone or something has trampled on your values.

When you live by your values, you feel happier and in sync with yourself. This includes your job: does your work align with your values? If on the other hand you do things that go against your own values, you might feel very strong emotions, depending on whether it is a core value or a less important value. This is because some values will be more important to you than others, and this can also change in different circumstances or different phases of life.

Some examples of values are: fairness, kindness, ambition, support, honesty, duty, creativity, freedom, making a difference, and so on. There are many values, so do look them up if you would like some inspiration. Interestingly, we may have strong reactions towards those we may perceive as having similar or different values from us, however even those sharing the same value might interpret it differently. What does freedom mean to you? What does it mean to the person next to you?

Activity

a. Make a list of your values: one or two words to title your value. You can look up value-words online for inspiration. Think about what drives you to make decisions, what you feel comfortable or uncomfortable doing and what the value behind that might be. Write at least 20 values.

b. Prioritise your values. Which are your core values (let's say between 3 and 5), which you *absolutely* live by and so on until the last one is ranked. It is up to you if you want to rank some at the same level, as long as you recognise for yourself what your core values are, the ones that are non-negotiable. If other values come to mind during this process, add them to your list.

c. Now describe the values on your list more at length. What do they mean to *you* specifically? Maybe "Honesty" means "To be honest and truthful to myself and others at all times" or maybe you will describe it differently.

d. Now that you're clear on what your values mean, think about where your life and work is aligned to your values. If you added "Service to others" as one of your values, where does your lived experience and actions reflect that? Maybe you spend some of your time volunteering, or perhaps you support or mentor people at work. Be specific about the kind of behaviours that are related to one or more of your values, and write down some examples.

e. Are there situations in which you feel you are behaving in contrast or without taking into account your values? What may the reason be for that, and what can you do about it?

f. Are there situations where you are not embodying a particular value? If so, what could you start doing to align with it? How does it make you feel to think about aligning to that value?

g. Take a wider look to your alignment. Do you feel like you are fairly aligned, well aligned or not so aligned to your values overall? Which areas are most aligned and which areas are least aligned? How do you feel about it? If you want to increase your overall alignment, which areas of your life can you address? Write some behaviours and actions that you commit to doing more of in the next month.

h. Make a list of 7 behaviours that are explicitly associated with some of your values, and commit to practising one a day for the next week. At the end of the week, repeat, and do this for the whole month.

i. At the end of the month, reflect and write down what has changed in the last month. How do you feel about yourself and your actions? Have you aligned your life and work more to your values? What have you learned from this experience? Any other thoughts?

Resources

Covey, Stephen – The 8th Habit: From Effectiveness to Greatness

DiMasi, Geoff – Is your work aligned with your values?

15. Read a good book

"If you only read the books that everyone else is reading, you can only think what everyone else is thinking." Haruki Murakami

I remember reading ages ago that when you are reading you can never be lonely. If reading a novel, you have the characters to keep you company. If you are reading a factual book, you have an opportunity to test out your own thinking and perhaps do further research etc. In short, books on the whole can be interactive and bring a lot of pleasure.

Books open up our world to so many possibilities and opportunities.

Activity

a. Think about the two books which have most impacted you and why.

b. Draw two circles. At the centre of the first circle write 'inner' and in the centre of the second write 'outer'. In the inner circle, write key words that describe how the books have impacted your inner world, e.g. the way you think, and do similarly in the outer circle, e.g. what you do differently as a result of how these books have impacted you.

Resources

Krashen, Stephen – The Power Of Research: Insights From The Research

Improvement Pill – Benefits Of Reading

Improvement Pill – Benefits Of Reading

16. Notice, moment to moment, how you're feeling

"I suppose I've always done my share of crying, especially when there's no other way to contain my feelings. I know that men ain't supposed to cry, but I think that's wrong. Crying's always been a way for me to get things out which are buried deep, deep down. When I sing, I often cry. Crying is feeling, and feeling is being human. Oh yes, I cry." Ray Charles

This is really important for our emotional, physical and psychological wellbeing.

Opening to oneself can be really rewarding in understanding who you are completely. Asking questions of yourself can really help with this. Here is a selection of questions.

Activity

a. Where am I, emotionally and physically? How am I feeling?

b. What am I doing that helps or hinders me?

c. What skills do I have that will help change how I'm thinking and feeling right now?

d. What's important to me? What's my big `why'? What is my purpose?

e. Who am I at my core?

f. What am I here for?

Resources

Sincero, Jen et al. – You Are A Badass: How To Stop Doubting Your Greatness And Start Living An Awesome Life

Robbins, Tony – Feeling lost? How To Find Yourself Again

17. Spend time in reflection

"It's your reaction to adversity, not adversity itself that determines how your life's story will develop." Dieter F. Uchtdorf

Reflection is a great way to learn and improve. It enhances awareness and can help you work on yourself. Self-reflection can be done, for example, by writing things down in a journal, so that you give yourself the time to process your thoughts around the topic you want to explore.

One great advantage of self-reflection is the gift of hindsight. Looking back at a situation that didn't work out the way you wanted to, for example, in hindsight you could reflect on what you did well, and what you could have done even better, so that you are prepared for next time.

Activity

a. Pen and paper at hand, think about a situation in which you didn't have the impact you wanted.

b. Write down in 2 columns what went well and what didn't.

c. Add in both columns the things *you* did, i.e. the actions that contributed to both outcomes. Be fair to yourself and populate both columns.

d. Do you notice anything you could do differently next time? Note that down at the bottom of the page.

e. Congratulate yourself on what you did well and think about how you can keep that up next time.

Resources

Peterson, Jordan – 12 Rules for Life: An Antidote to Chaos

Siegel, Dan – Time In: Reflection, Relationships and Resilience at the Heart of Internal Education

18. Break your worries down and check for facts

"On the other side of a storm is the strength that comes from having navigated through it. Raise your sail and begin." Gregory S. Williams

Have you ever mulled over thoughts and worries more than you needed to? Have you felt like you couldn't let go of negative thinking, and it brought you into a spiral of negativity that was hard to escape? If so, you're not alone! Worrying about things is very common and can be healthy, as long as you're still in the driving seat. When worries take over, they can be very disruptive and affect your mental wellbeing.

Something that might help you move away from the spiral of worrying is breaking your worries down and looking at the dry facts. It is also useful to distinguish between those things that are under your control, and those that are not. Is it worth it to worry about things that you can't control? Or could you instead focus your attention on actions you can take based on what you can control?

Activity

a. Pen and paper at hand, draw your Worry. What does it look like?

b. What is your worry saying to you? Write those words verbatim inside a dialogue bubble.

c. Among these bubble-words, highlight in red the unhelpful ones and in green the potentially useful ones? For example, if my worry is telling me: "I have never faced this issue before", "I don't know how to do this", "this problem needs solving" and “oh dear, what if I can’t figure it out?”, I would highlight in red all the bubbles except “this problem needs solving”, which I would highlight in green.

d. Starting with the red bubbles, fact-check them. Is it really true that “I have never faced this issue before”? Think back to all the similar challenges you have faced in the past, and how you were able to overcome them. Now write another sentence in a different colour, that is more accurate. This could be something like: “I haven’t experienced this particular issue before, however I have dealt with similar issues before and I was able to solve them” – then go into detail and write down for yourself what those issues were, when they took place and all the things you did to successfully overcome them. Similarly, is it really true that “you can’t do this”? What you are doing here is challenging your self-limiting beliefs by referring back to real examples that will help you see how you *can* face this.

e. Beware of the “what if” thoughts, which are based on imagination of future outcomes that haven’t actually happened and don’t need to happen in the way that worries you. Replace them with an affirming thought, for example “I will figure this out when I focus my attention on the issue.”

f. Add more affirming thoughts that can reframe the unhelpful ones and be in larger numbers than the unhelpful ones. These are thoughts that are more helpful to you because they are: confidence-boosting and energy-boosting *and* they are true. They can start with: “I can do it because…” (add all the reasons why you know you have the skills to do it). The mindset has now shifted from what worries you to what you can do about it.

g. Now write down in a different colour all the things that you *can* do about this problem, those things that are under your control and in your power to do. These can include asking someone for help and thinking outside the box – perhaps something different from the norm but effective. Now you are focusing on action and generating ideas. Are you feeling more empowered yet?

h. Now draw your Power (as opposed to your Worry), which is strengthened by the affirming bubbles that you have written so far. What does it look like? Can you identify with your Power rather than your Worry?

Resources

Greitens, Eric – Resilience: Hard-Won Wisdom for Living a Better Life

Gottlieb, Lori – How Changing Your Story Can Change Your Life

19. Journal about what is exciting

"When I dare to be powerful, to use my strength in the service of my vision, then it becomes less and less important whether I am afraid." Audre Lorde

When you start writing about what is exciting and nourishing and lovely in your work and life, it is a process that can be deeply satisfying as well as creative. You can unleash your imagination and your visioning of an exciting future ahead.

As you describe what is exciting, take time to delve into the juicy details and emotional aspects. Describe your feelings and let your thoughts and writing be driven by your passion. You might find yourself smiling in the process!

Activity

a. Pick a notebook that you can dedicate to exciting things and find a spot where you are comfortable to write. Give yourself at least 20 minutes to write without interruption. If in doubt about how to start…just start with the first thing that comes to mind.

b. Think about what makes you happy and why. How does it make you feel? Go into detail about your feelings and any physical sensations that arise when you think back to those moments, or even as you write.

c. If you want to focus on the future, bring your mind to that future and what looks exciting from that standpoint. Envision what the future looks like: Where are you? Who are you with? What exciting things are you doing? Imagine it as if it were already happening.

d. Once you stop writing, take a moment to breathe. What have you noticed from this exercise? Note down your thoughts as they come. Notice if there are any actions you want to take as a result of completing this activity. Write them down.

Resources

Spiegel, Cyndie – A Year of Positive Thinking: Daily Inspiration, Wisdom, and Courage

Le, Ann – 30 journaling writing prompts + ideas

20. Change the way you are thinking about a negative situation

"My go-to phrase I say to myself when I feel stuck, overwhelmed, or like I don't quite measure up is: 'All I can do, is all I can do, and all I can do is enough." Emily Madill

Consider a difficult situation in your life. Recognising that it is sometimes hard to take our head out of the downsides, consider a different perspective. What might the upsides of the situation be?

Activity

a. Consider reframing what the situation might mean to you. What could it mean if you chose to look at the situation differently?

b. Take a look at the language you use to describe the situation – how does this language make you feel? Consider moving to a more empowering language, recognising that language creates your reality.

Resources

Moore, Rob and Murray, John – Start Now, Get Perfect Later

Ledgerwood, Alison – Getting Stuck In The Negatives (And How To Get Unstuck)

21. Write down your mental needs

"Resilience is based on compassion for ourselves as well as compassion for others." Sharon Salzberg

Taking care of your mental health is just as important as taking care of your physical health. Thinking about it, talking about it, and taking care of it regularly is important to stay healthy.

We are all different, so needs will be varied. There are also high moments and low moments, which can vary too. Your focus and your needs will be unique to you and to your current circumstances.

Activity

a. Think about your patterns. Where does your mind typically go when you're nervous? When you're tired? When you're emotionally involved? What about when you're distracted?

b. Now think about what you might need in those situations. Where might you need to focus your mind instead, in order to be calm? Productive? Objective? Focused?

c. What might your mind need on a regular basis? What might it need when you're under pressure? Think about current situations you're struggling with: what might your mind need in those situations? What can you give your mind and how? Write yourself an action plan.

Resources

Reivich, Karen, & Shatte, Andrew – The Resilience Factor: 7 Keys to Finding Your Inner Strength and Overcoming Life's Hurdles

Mind, the mental health charity – How to relax | 8 relaxation tips for your mental health

22. Balance your work and life

"Thinking is easy, acting difficult, and to put one's thoughts into action, the most difficult thing in the world." Johann Wolfgang von Goethe

Work-life balance has become a mantra, but are they really two separated things? Work is a very important part of life – possibly what we spend most of our time doing. And life, well life is work in progress! Balance includes your level of happiness and sense of achievement.

You have many different roles, within and beyond your work. You are a member of your family, a partner, an expert of you-name-it and so on. You can identify not only in your job or role, but also in hobbies, passions and relationships. Different things bring out different qualities. Balance is the combination of balancing your roles, your needs, your time and your wants.

Activity

a. Draw a circle and divide it into 8 slices.

b. Add the following titles to each slice: Work, Health, Fitness, Family, Friends/Community Financial, Love/Relationships, Fun/Passions and Personal Development.

c. What areas are you satisfied with and where would you like to improve? Think more in detail about each area and note down how happy you are from 1 (very low) to 10 (very high) in that area.

d. Also note down how much time you dedicate to that area and what activities or people populate it at the moment.

e. Looking at your pie chart, what do you notice overall? Take another look, what else do you notice?

f. What are some actions you would like to take in the areas you want to improve. Write 3 things you can do starting tomorrow in each area of improvement. Be kind to yourself: everyone is on a learning curve and everyone is evolving.

g. Be ambitious. How are the changes you want to make in some areas going to help you go in the direction you want? How can you keep yourself accountable?

Resources

Pink, Daniel – When: The Scientific Secrets of Perfect Timing

Marsh, Nigel – How to make work-life balance work

23. Journal about what is worrying you

"During difficult times, an important resiliency step is being able to express your feelings in healthy ways. You can't make feelings go away, but you can move through them." *Al Siebert*

Journaling is a great way to process thoughts and emotions, make sense of them, and oftentimes find helpful insights. It is a mindful exercise that helps cope with stressors you may experience in life, and also helps see things more clearly. Many find it to be a liberating experience.

Expressive writing is the art of sitting down and putting what is going on with you on paper, in a journal that is written by you only for yourself. This free-flow of thoughts does not need to be bound by logic, structure or grammar – it is simply a way for you to express yourself without judgment and without a particular goal.

Activity

a. Find a comfortable place to sit with a journal, and give yourself at least 20 minutes to write without interruptions or distractions. If you want, you can use a timer.

b. Pick something that has been worrying you and start writing. Put down on paper any thoughts and emotions as they flow freely through your mind. Keep going until the 20 minutes are up.

c. When the time is up, you can set aside more time if you want to carry on writing, or you can stop. Once you stop writing, set the journal aside and take a breath. How are you feeling now?

Note that down for yourself and take a break from your journal – go do something else.

d. When you come back from your break, look back at what you wrote earlier. Has it brought new insight? What ideas have emerged as a result of writing? What feelings? Has this helped you and if so, how?

e. If any ideas have emerged that you want to act upon, note down the most important points in a nutshell, and your next steps.

Resources

Lisson, Lisa – Resilience: Navigating Life, Loss, and the Road to Success

D'Avella, Matt – What I Learned by Journaling for 30 Days

24. Accept what is and focus on what you're going to do about it

"Accept what is, let go of what was, and have faith in what will be." Sonia Ricotti

When difficult situations arise, maybe situations that cannot be rectified or are nobody's fault, or imposed changes that you have to go through not by choice, often the first reaction is denial. There is an emotional curve people often go through that is similar to the 5 stages of grief: denial, bargaining, anger, depression and acceptance.

Denial is when you don't really believe it's happening: you are still in a state of shock and disbelief. Anger is when you look for the culprit and point fingers, so you can blame someone. Bargaining is when you are still mulling over it, thinking "if only" you had done something differently, or "what if" it had happened another day. Depression is when you finally allow yourself to feel what you're feeling in the present. It is ok to be sad, at loss or not know what to do. Finally, Acceptance is when you accept that things have changed and realise that you may need to change some things too in order to adjust. This leads to positive action you can take for yourself.

Activity

a. Think about an imposed change that has impacted your life at work or at home.

b. Draw on a piece of paper your unique emotional curve. This may or may not mirror the 5 stages of grief. Make sure you name your emotions specifically. These are not what you *thought* as you went through it, but how you *felt*.

c. Look back at your curve, and think about what helped you and what would have helped you further through each stage. This could include particular thoughts (thinking about the change in a different way) and/or particular actions (for example talking to someone or taking a break from something).

d. With this knowledge, do you find that your curve is recurring with other changes that happened in your life? What would you take from your previous reflection that might help you deal with changes that might occur in the future? What will help you reach acceptance and move forward?

Resources

Salzgeber, Jonas – The Little Book of Stoicism: Timeless Wisdom to Gain Resilience, Confidence, and Calmness

Hone, Lucy – The three secrets of resilient people

25. Find time to play: what gives you pleasure?

"A smile is a curve that sets everything straight." Phyllis Diller

Unstructured playtime is really important in child development. Why do we forget about playing and playfulness as adults? This is baffling, because playfulness is linked to creativity, enjoyment and motivation.

We learn more when we are enjoying what we are doing, rather than not enjoying it. So, what is it that you enjoy doing? What does play look like for you, and do you spend enough time playing?

Activity

a. Make a list of all the things you enjoy doing that constitute playtime for you. This could range from playing board games with friends to practicing a hobby to learning something new.

b. Looking back at your list, which of those things are you currently doing and which ones are you not doing but would like to engage with? How frequently are you engaging with the current play-activities? Are you happy with that frequency?

c. Overall, do you feel happy with your playtime, or would you increase it? If you feel like an increase would do you good, which activities in your list would you pick out? When and how would you fit them in your calendar?

d. Think about the benefits of your playful activities on your overall wellbeing. Make a list of benefits so that you can see the extent of their impact on your life.

e. Narrow the activities down to the ones you can realistically make time for, and plan for them by putting them in your schedule!

Resources

Gilbert, Elizabeth – Big Magic: Creative Living Beyond Fear

Roering, Dena – Playful Grownups Overcoming Adversity

26. Connect Thoughts-Feelings-Actions

"Turn your wounds into wisdom." Oprah Winfrey

Thoughts, feelings and actions / behaviours are deeply interconnected and affect each other in the blink of an eye. Most people experience self-talk which often times is self-sabotaging rather than helpful. What you think and feel *will* determine your behaviours – often unconsciously.

Working on the relationship between the thoughts, feelings and actions constitutes the basis of cognitive behavioural therapy (CBT) and related approaches. These approaches help people become more self-aware of their patterns and devise coping mechanisms that better serve their needs.

Activity

a. Draw a triangle on a piece of paper. Label the top angle T for Thoughts, the bottom right angle F for Feelings and the bottom left angle A for actions.

b. Think of something you have been struggling with. It could be a difficult relationship or getting your voice heard in meetings. Think about the type of situations where the struggle has been recurring, and pick one specific situation you would like to focus on.

c. Describe the context of the situation and the event. If it is about a difficult relationship at work, for example, pick the last difficult conversation you had with that person and zoom in on that.

d. In that specific instance, what thoughts were going through your head? Write them down verbatim (in quotation marks) near the T for Thoughts. For example, you might find yourself thinking "X doesn't like me" or "what's the use of talking", and so on. Write down those specific thoughts in that specific instance.

e. How did those thoughts leave you feeling? Go back with your mind to the feelings you had in that moment, and write them down near the F for Feelings. You might have experienced anger or maybe frustration. You name it.

f. What did you end up doing next? Be specific about both what you did (your actions) and how you did it (the nuances of your behaviour). Include your body language and non-verbal communication. For example, if you were thinking "what's the use" and feeling frustrated, you may have snapped "whatever" at the person in a loud voice, and then regretted it.

g. Can you see the cycle happening?

h. Now draw the figure of a person outside the triangle and the title 'Come Across'. Looking back at your triangle, how do you think your behaviour affected the way you came across to that person, and perhaps to other people who witnessed the conversation?

i. Now look at ways in which you may possibly reframe your thoughts. Perhaps, in that context, you might park the unhelpful thoughts and think something like: "Maybe X will hear me out" or "I have a good point to make". Think back to your situation and write down verbatim what more useful alternative thoughts you could have had.

j. With those thoughts in mind, populate the possible different feelings these thoughts would evoke, and how then this would affect your behaviour. Would you have perhaps acted differently, said different words, in a different way? What words in which way? Also notice how your body language might be different.

k. You could also start with your behaviour. How might you change your behaviour in a way that serves you better, so that you don't act on impulse? For example, instead of snapping and raising your voice, what else could you challenge yourself to do in that situation, that would lead to a better outcome?

Resources

Branch, Rhena – Cognitive Behavioural Therapy For Dummies

Pinnacle of Man – Cognitive Behavioral Therapy (CBT) Simply Explained

27. Notice your patterns

"Don't Trust Words. Even Question Actions. But Never Doubt Patterns." Nicole Zimmerman

Everyone has patterns of behaviour: these are ways in which you automatically repeat what you do without really thinking about it. Often times, your behaviour becomes so automatic, that you are not conscious about it anymore, until someone or something happens that makes you take notice.

Patterns are great ways to short-cut our actions, without having to rethink everything from scratch, and often times they work very well for you. However, sometimes patterns end up working *against* you, even in the form of self-sabotage. Does that ring a bell? When you are unhappy with how something is going for you, look out for your patterns. Once you are aware of them, you can make a choice to change for the better.

Activity

a. Think about something that 'went wrong' and how you dealt with it. Have there been other similar instances, and was the way you dealt with them similar? What was your recurring behaviour in those situations?

b. Once you found some recurring events in which your behaviour was working against you, be more specific about it. What were the details of your behaviour: the timing of it, the intensity and your thoughts before you acted?

c. When you are clear about it, sum it up in the following sentence and fill in the blanks: "When ……. happens (the event type), I tend to ……. (your action/behaviour), which in turns leads to ………(outcome)”. Review it so that it is an accurate representation of when your automatic behaviour happens.

d. Think about downsides of your behaviour and write them down.

e. Think about why that behaviour might have become your automatic one: what is the need that you express beneath it? Perhaps it comes in handy in different situations?

f. Now think about how you could shift the behaviour that doesn’t work, in order to better respond to that particular type of situation. What could you replace it with, that works better in that situation and *also* meets your needs?

g. Start practicing the shift in behaviour with full awareness. You now know when those situations are likely to arise and how you want to improve the way you deal with them. Practice as much as you can so that it becomes easier for you to control how you want to respond to those situations.

h. Repeat the process to address other unhelpful patterns.

Resources

Zahariades, Damon – Small Habits Revolution: 10 Steps To Transforming Your Life Through The Power Of Mini Habits!

Eurich, Tasha – Increase your self-awareness with one simple fix

28. Be Perfectly Imperfect

"To banish imperfection is to destroy expression, to check exertion, to paralyze vitality." John Ruskin

There is no such thing as perfection, and even if there were, it would be subjective. What I consider perfect might not be the same as what you consider perfect. Think about how this applies to work. If you are a perfectionist, you will have set your bar very high, though your "average" might actually be high for the rest of us!

If you are a perfectionist, what you're doing is probably setting yourself up for failure. Think about where you put your high bars at work or in other situations (relationship requirements included!). What are pros of setting a high bar? What are the downsides? For some things, it is paramount to expect and want a certain level of quality, however for other things, what is ok in your eyes might just be what is needed. Think about work: what kind of time do you need for something to be perfect according to your standards, and what kind of time would you need to simply get it done in an appropriate and acceptable way?

Ultimately, if you think of yourself, your qualities and traits, people will love and remember what is "imperfect" about you, which is what makes you so special and unique. You don't need to adhere to an image of perfection that is often set out by corporations and society. Who you are is perfectly imperfect and wonderful as it is!

Activity

a. Are you a perfectionist? Rate yourself on perfectionism between 1 (very low) and 10 (very high). This may vary depending on certain tasks and activities, so feel free to be more detailed.

b. List the pros and cons of your perfectionism. What has it enabled you to do well, and what has it prevented you from doing / doing well?

c. Where do you think "acceptable" and "good" lie on your scale between "disaster" and "perfect"? Populate the scale with other words too, so that you can see it as a spectrum.

d. According to your populated scale, what would be the lowest acceptable point for you and for others in that situation. For example, if you are writing a report and your level of excellence includes all types of minute details, consider what "good" means for your boss or workers, what level of detail the task actually requires to be considered well done, and where that is on your scale. Maybe your "good" is their "excellent"!

e. Consider how doing something well without going over the top might benefit you. Perhaps it will save you considerable time that you can dedicate to other tasks. What are the positives?

Resources

Sunim, Haemin – Love for Imperfect Things: How to Accept Yourself in a World Striving for Perfection

Stahl, Ashley – How to Figure Out What You Really Want

29. Challenge self-limiting beliefs

"You begin to fly when you let go of self-limiting beliefs and allow your mind and aspirations to rise to greater heights." Brian Tracy

Beliefs are assumptions you make on people or situations based on the experience you have had before, or what you have heard or been taught in the past, starting from childhood. These assumptions can include biases towards others, and also limiting beliefs towards yourself.

Focusing on self-limiting beliefs, these are things you believe about yourself that might be holding you back. For example, if you believe you won't succeed in a particular project, this belief will have an active impact on what happens next (particularly your attitude and behaviours) by increasing the likelihood of not succeeding: a self-fulfilling prophecy!

Activity

a. Pen and paper at hand, write down 3 situations in which you are struggling. Perhaps you don't feel confident about yourself, or you feel stuck. Maybe you haven't quite pinpointed it, but you feel that something has been holding you back from achieving your goals and moving forward.

b. Describe in more detail what has been holding you back, not just externally (external obstacles) but also internally (mindset, thought process, etc). Beware of pointing fingers! If you find yourself blaming others, try to suspend judgment and simply list all the obstacles you have come across.

c. You can't change other people, so the tools you have at your disposal are analysis and choice around how you can change *your* thoughts and behaviour. It may seem counterintuitive, but if *you* change, everything else changes around you. You might not know how, but you *will* have an impact. So, what you're going to do now is focus on yourself only.

d. With that in mind, think about the specific unhelpful thoughts you had in those 3 situations, and write them down verbatim (in between quotation marks), just as if you were writing down your internal dialogue as it happens. For example, you might catch yourself thinking "This isn't going to work", or "They will judge me", or "I can't do it".

e. Thinking about what beliefs about yourself may be lying underneath these thoughts. Often self-limiting beliefs involve believing you're not good enough. Try digging a bit deeper to uncover what might be driving those unhelpful thoughts, and what past life experiences may have led you to believe them.

f. You know these beliefs are not helping you, so it is time to take back charge of your life and move forward. Pick out the thoughts that are unhelpful, and write down alternative thoughts that you will benefit more from. This means reframing those thoughts so that they are helpful to you rather than unhelpful. For example, find all the reasons why you "can do it" and give yourself evidence of it.

g. You will find that your self-limiting beliefs are often unfounded. Debunk those myths and tell yourself what you want to believe. Tell yourself that you want to believe in yourself so that things that felt impossible before may become possible. Find the words to say to yourself what beliefs you are debunking, and how you want to reframe them in a way that is helpful to you moving forward.

h. In essence, when a belief or thought about yourself is limiting you, challenge it! Find your way forward.

Resources

Meurisse, Thibaut – Master Your Destiny: A Practical Guide to Rewrite Your Story and Become the Person You Want to Be

Majd, Pari – Can You Change Your Perception in Four Minutes?

30. Live with meaning

"Freedom isn't about having permission to do whatever we want... it's about having the courage to do whatever fills our life with meaning." Bill Crawford

The world goes on and so does every day, but what is a day worth if it has no meaning? Those who have survived terrible life and death situations often relay that it is not enough to just 'survive'. Survival is not a strong enough motivation to actually survive. We need more.

Holocaust survivor Viktor Frankl explained that what helped him survive his ordeal was finding meaning to it. Why was he actually there and what could he do with that? Finding meaning was something no one could take away from him. He was driven by the will to make it out of the camp and write about his experiences, so that history wouldn't repeat itself in the future. This gave him the strength not only to survive, but also to go on and create 'Meaning Therapy'. Meaning is part of the core elements of resilience.

Activity

a. Find a quiet space to reflect and write without interruption.

b. Think about your past experiences and how far you've come. Connect the dots: what was the meaning of those experiences? List some things that you had no idea about when you started them, and became clearer later in your life. How did those experiences shape your present?

c. Tell yourself 3 reasons why you're here, on this Earth. What contributions do you want to make to the world? Think about how you would like to serve a higher cause, beyond your individual satisfaction.

d. If you feel like you have one (or more) vocations, how would you describe it / them?

d. Connect those 3 reasons and vocations to your values. What are the core values that emerge?

e. How aligned to your vocations and values are you in your current life and work? Rate yourself from 1 (very low alignment) to 10 (very high alignment).

f. If you want to improve your alignment, what are some things you can do? How will they be meaningful to you? Choose some actions you will commit to over the year, and stick to them. Note down what you notice in a journal throughout the year.

g. Review this work in a year's time. What have you noticed? How will you move forward to live your life with meaning in the coming year?

Resources

Sinek, Simon – Start With Why: How Great Leaders Inspire Everyone To Take Action

Steger, Michael – What Makes Life Meaningful

Taking Charge & Action

31. Stay positively focused

"Lack of direction, not lack of time, is the problem. We all have twenty-four-hour days." Zig Ziglar

Recognising and acknowledging your successes is a very effective confidence booster. It is often easy to focus only on what has gone wrong and beat ourselves up for it. Instead, wouldn't you want to be fair with yourself, in the same way you would with a good friend?

Looking back at your successes also gives you the tools to analyse what skills and resources you put into place in that situation. It is a great tool for personal belief and empowerment.

Activity

a. Identify three issues that you have concerns about and write down at least seven ways you can address each of those concerns.

b. Put in place your plan of action to address those concerns.

Resources

Dweck, Carol, & Dunne, Bernadette et al – Mindset

Brown, Les – Power of a Positive Thinking

32. Take action to address your situation

"The path to success is to take massive, determined action." Tony Robbins

What is your situation? Do you fully know the who, what, why, when, where and how of the situation you are in? Are you within your comfort zone or outside of it? What do you feel about your situation? In what ways, if any, do you want your situation to change?

Activity

a. Draw a quadrant and write `Strengths' (things that are good about the situation), in the top left-hand box, `Weaknesses` (things that you don't like about the situation, things that are not going well and could be different) in the top right-hand box, `Opportunities` (things that you can take advantage of to make the situation better) in the bottom left-hand box and `Threats` (things that perhaps are on the horizon that could make the situation worse) in the bottom-right hand box.

b. Undertake a SWOT analysis of your situation.

c. Consider how you might enhance the Strengths and Opportunities factors, whilst diminishing the Weaknesses and Threats factors.

Resources

Sinek, Simon – Start With Why: How Great Leaders Inspire Everyone To Take Action

Garguilo, Steve – The Science Of Taking Action

33. Focus your mind on solutions

"She stood in the storm and when the wind did not blow her way, she adjusted her sails." Elizabeth Edwards

There is a matter you want to solve and you are at a loss for ideas and solutions. Well, you're not alone! Focusing on 'the problem' is in many ways useful, however you also need to develop a solutions-oriented mindset.

Thinking about solutions can be an incredibly creative and energy-boosting process. One of the techniques you can use to think about solutions creatively is brainstorming. While this is often done with a group of people, we will explore here the art of self-brainstorming.

Activity

a. Find a quiet place to write. Dedicate 20 minutes to this exercise without interruption.

b. Make a list of the issues you want to brainstorm and generate ideas on. Prioritise them and start considering the first issue.

c. Make sure you are clear about what you want to generate ideas on. Then reword it in a way that sounds like an open question, such as "ways to" or "how to". For example, if the issue is that your financial situation is not satisfactory, you could word this as "ways to create more income", or "how to improve my financial situation". This will stimulate your brain to think about solutions.

d. On another page, draw a circle and write your "how to" or "ways to" in the middle. Draw some lines coming out of the circle: at the end of each line you will be noting down a solution. You will be drawing as many lines as the solutions you can think of.

e. Set your timer to 5 minutes and start writing all the ideas that come to mind, even your wildest thoughts, without judging them and without going into detail. Each idea should be very short, only a few words long, and once you've written it, swiftly move on to the next idea.

f. When the 5 minutes are over, pick your top 5 ideas and circle them.

g. Analyse each idea and provide more detail. This is the time to look at things like feasibility, obstacles and practicalities, to test the idea's soundness.

h. Now take a look at the other ideas and analyse them too, no matter how ambitious they may look. Perhaps there is an out-of-the-box solution hidden there.

i. Having explored your ideas; which ones do you think you can start applying? Make a plan that is specific, measurable and time bound.

j. Repeat the process for the other issues you had noted on your list.

Resources

Goleman, Daniel – Focus: The Hidden Driver of Excellence

Owunwanne, Enyinne – Got problem? Think solution.

34. Say 'no' to overwhelm

"Sometimes when you're overwhelmed by a situation - when you're in the darkest of darkness - that's when your priorities are reordered." Phoebe Snow

Linked to 'saying yes to help', overwhelm is real. It interrupts your flow of life – you stop sleeping through the night, your thought patterns become more problem than solutions-focused. If you smoke or drink, you might tend to do that more, and overindulge on certain foods etc.

Activity

a. Take a look at what you are feeling overwhelmed by and interrogate the overwhelm. I use the word interrogate very deliberately here because I really want you to confront what may be a familiar pattern for you. Your answers to the following questions, interrogating overwhelm may help:

I. What have you come to teach me?

II. What do I need to stop doing, start doing, do less of or more of?

III. When I let this overwhelm go, how will my life be different?

b. To the extent the responses to your questions on overwhelm make sense to you, take the appropriate action steps to move out of your overwhelm.

Resources

Aron, Elaine – The Highly Sensitive Person: How To Survive And Thrive When The World Overwhelms You

Robbins, Mel – How To Stop Feeling Overwhelmed

35. Use the power of intention

"Failure will never overtake me if my determination to succeed is strong enough." *Og Mandino*

According to the Cambridge dictionary, intention is something you want and plan to do. What are your intentions? There is also a subtler meaning If you think of the act of setting an intention, which has to do with the power of your mind.

You can set for yourself and intention of *being* in a certain way, so that you come across effectively. For example, you can set the intention of being calm and poised when you walk into a particular meeting. Or, perhaps, you want to come across as professional and knowledgeable. When you set an intention, your voice, body language and words will naturally accompany it.

Activity

a. Think of an upcoming situation (a meeting, an interview, a conversation, etc) where you feel your confidence might be wobbly.

b. Place a camera in the room you're in so that you can video-record yourself.

c. Make a list of words that represent how you *don't* want to come across. For example: bored, unprofessional, nervous.

d. Now make a list of words that represent how you do want to come across. For example: knowledgeable, approachable, concise.

e. Pick one word from the “don’t want” list, set that as an intention in your head, and record yourself for 10-15 second introducing yourself with that “vibe”, in the situation you thought of. You don’t have to prepare a script: just introduce yourself with that “way of being”.

f. Now pick one word from the “want” list, set that as an intention in your head, and record yourself for 10-15 second introducing yourself with that “vibe”, in the situation you thought of. You don’t have to prepare a script: just introduce yourself with that “way of being” set as an intention.

g. Compare the video-recordings. Did you notice any changes in the words you used, the tone of voice, your body movements and body language?

h. Now that you have seen the power of setting an intention, practice the same introduction using different words from the list of the intentions you want to set for yourself. You can video-record yourself and watch yourself back, or ask a friend to give you feedback on how you came across.

g. Now that you know you can set an intention for yourself and have an impact on others, how are you going to use this power?

Resources

Covey, Stephen – How to Develop Your Personal Mission Statement

McCulla, Colleen – The power of intention

36. Stay in control of those things you can control and don't worry about the rest

"Do the one thing you think you cannot do. Fail at it. Try again. Do better the second time. The only people who never tumble are those who never mount the high wire." Oprah Winfrey

Have you ever found yourself in a complete state of worry? Worrying about everything: family, home, finances, where to from here and any number of other things?

The truth is, we can only control what we can control. Some things are completely out of our hands. In those moments, consider what it is you *can* do. The options are likely to include: tackle the situation (come up with an action plan); accept that there's nothing you can do about it and watch the situation play out; identify what aspects of the situation you do have control over and who or what can help you.

Activity

Create a 'force field' analysis.

a. Find a blank page in your journal. At the top of the page write down the issue you are grappling with.

b. Write each of the following scenarios in a box labelling each as follows:
On the left-hand side of the page, write down the worst-case scenario, in the middle of the page the actual situation and on the right-hand side, write down the end goal / ideal outcome.

c. Beneath the boxes, draw a line down the centre of the page. In the top right-hand column write down 'helping factors' – what will help to resolve the situation and in the top left-hand column write down 'hindering factors' – those forces that are not helping the situation and/or are making it worse.

d. Develop a plan of action to eliminate the hindering factors and a plan to capitalise on the helping forces.

Resources

Murphy, Joseph – The Power Of Your Subconscious Mind

Fearless Soul – 7 Things You Can Control Which Will Make A Huge Difference In Your Life

37. State the problem and rehearse the solution

"Worrying is to rehearse the problem without a solution."
Thomas Dexter Jakes

The recommendation here is to state the problem and rehearse the solution, meaning to thoroughly understand the problem and then throw all of your efforts into rehearsing/finding the solution. This means it is likely that you'll come up with a myriad of ways to deal with any situation and can choose the solution that most fits the issue at hand.

Activity

a. Identify a situation you want to address and make sure you understand it fully.

b. When you understand it fully, pay no more attention to understanding the situation and instead, throw all of your attention into coming up with at least seven possible solutions to address the situation.

c. Start rehearsing these solutions right away. Rehearsing means practising and implementing. When and how are you going to apply your solutions?

Resources

Ortner, Nick – The Tapping Solution: A Revolutionary System For Stress Free Living

Gill, Mel – <u>Uncommon Sense: Moving From A Problem Focused To A Solutions Focused Mindset</u>

38. Adapt to the current environment

"When your clarity meets your conviction and you apply action to the equation, your world will begin to transform before your eyes." Lisa Nichols

In adapting to your current environment, it's important to be flexible in your approach. So, what does this mean in practice? Understand the environment and why the potential need for adaptation. Understand what adaptation means in your given context. Be flexible in your approach as to the outcome. Recognise that you may well have varied responses to the adaptations that need to be made, from shock through to acceptance and a myriad of emotions in between.

Possible adaptations could be in the form of mindset, organisational change, rules, regulations, laws, etc.

Activity

a. Consider if you are open to embracing change and how you might make the most of a given situation.

b. Establish what you consider the pros and cons of the new situation.

c. What actions will you commit to in relation to making these changes?

Resources

Peterson, Jordan B – 12 Rules For Life: An Antidote To Chaos

Van Warmerdam, Gary – How To Change Beliefs

39. Step back from getting involved with drama

"Isn't it kind of silly to think that tearing someone else down builds you up?" Sean Covey

Some people just live for an argument. They don't even need any provocation. Stay away from those people. They will argue with you just because they can – it feeds some need in them to be engaged and stay engaged in drama. The extent to which this doesn't serve you, stay away from this type of interaction. It takes your energy and wastes your time.

Activity

a. Stay away from drama and do something better with your time instead.

b. Make a list of the things that you really want to occupy your time and schedule some of these in your calendar.

Resources

Vanzant, Iyanla – Get Over It

Singh, Lilly – Only Unhappy Put Others Down

40. Make a decision to stay positive

"When faced with a decision, choose the path that feeds your soul." Dorothy Mendoza Row

Staying positive, I do believe is a choice. Not that there aren't things that may pull you to the other side, it's just that you can look at the situation and decide how to deal with it. I'm not saying it's possible to be 'happy clappy' a 100% of the time, I'm just saying, when we take more control of ourselves – our mind, body and spiritual life – this provides us with more choices.

Activity

a. Think about some fond memories you've had in your life.

b. Make them more vivid, colourful, bright. See, hear and feel what made those experiences so happy. Sit in this energy for a while.

c. Do this activity often, two or three times a week. Stay in the positivity of the moment and notice how this energy can help you to positively focus on other areas of your life.

Resources

Nichols, Lisa – Abundance Now: Amplify Your Life and Achieve Prosperity Today

Winfrey, Oprah – How To Give And Receive Positive Karma

41. Face the situation and take action to address it

"Come to the edge," he said.
"We can't, we're afraid!" they responded.
"Come to the edge," he said.
"We can't, we will fall!" they responded.
"Come to the edge," he said.
And so, they came.
And he pushed them.
And they flew.
Guillaume Apollinaire

No matter how hard the situation is, you can face it. No matter how hard the situation is, you can deal with it. Look at the situation as it is, for what it is. You can seek to understand what this situation has come to teach you.

Activity

a. Look at the pros and cons of a situation.

b. Brainstorm the myriad ways the issue could be addressed.

c. Seek your own wise counsel as well as the wise counsel of others whom you trust.

Resources

Vanzant. Iyana – Peace From Broken Pieces: How To Get Through What You Are Going Through

Tracy, Brian – How To Turn A Negative Situation Into A Positive One

42. Train your brain to become more resilient

"It is when the discomfort strikes that they realise a strong mind is the most powerful weapon of all." *Chrissie Wellington*

Our brains can become more resilient through our genetics as well as through the circumstances of our growth during our formative years.

Levels of stress in our lives can also be a key determinant for how we respond to life, whether it be fight, flight, freeze or face. Too much stress on an ongoing basis weakens our resilience.

Activity

Take a look at some brain resilience videos to address how you might increase your levels of resilience through activating receptors in your brain. If you need more support, seek medical help from appropriate therapists.

Resources

Morin, Amy – 13 Things Mentally Strong People Don't Do: Take Back Your Power, Embrace Change, Face Your Fears, and Train Your Brain for Happiness and Success

Alberta Family Wellness Initiative – Brains: Journey To Resilience

Support & Community

43. Make a list of all the people who are in your support system

"Nourishing relationships is the single most universally agreed-upon feature of the good life." Daniel Goleman

No one is invincible. We all need people in our lives: people you can count on, mentors and trusted friends. Sometimes you don't even know whom you can count on until during difficult times. Sometimes you might feel like no one is willing to help, but is that really true, or is your thinking wrapped up in difficult feelings? You may well be surprised by the number of people who are happy and willing to help.

Asking for support is like giving someone the gift of your trust. You are trusting them to help you. This is such a lovely and bonding thing to do. If you flip it around: have you ever felt that glowing sensation of being trusted and wanting to be helpful when someone you care about asked *you* for help?

Activity

a. Make the following lists with the names of people you would go to for different types of support:

1. Encouragement
2. Honest feedback
3. When you simply want to be listened to
4. Help thinking through a problem
5. Mentorship in the workplace
6. Expressing your emotions openly
7. Understanding and empathy
8. Help with focusing on solutions
9. Anything else that is helpful to you

b. Looking back at your list: are there any surprises? How does it make you feel?

c. Note what you appreciate about each person on your list. How can you let them know they are appreciated? Have a think and then…do it! It is lovely to nurture your support system.

Resources

Pigott, Judy – Personal Safety Nets: Getting Ready for Life's Inevitable Changes and Challenges

The Mental Health Foundation – Relationships: the missing piece of the wellbeing puzzle

44. Don't be afraid to ask for help

"You recover better when you tell your family, a friend, or a support group what you are feeling. If you'd like them just to listen and not problem solve while you talk, let them know. If you want some suggestions and coaching on what to do, let them know that." Al Siebert

Have you ever felt like you didn't want to burden someone else with your problems or needs, much less ask them to help you? Perhaps you felt you were undeserving of that help, or you justified not asking for help by saying to yourself you didn't want to burden or worry other people?

Resilient people know when to lean on others to ask them for the support they need. It is ok to feel overwhelmed and under pressure. It is ok to *feel*. You don't need to put on a strong mask all the time. That is what trusted friends and colleagues are there for, and if you let them, others may surprise you too. All you need to give back is an enthusiastic 'Thank You'!

Remember that support is also offered by qualified professionals, such as coaches, counsellors, and others, depending on your needs.

Activity

a. Write down what is currently making you feel overwhelmed. What is it that is difficult to cope with? Perhaps you are juggling a number of pressures at home and at work, or maybe a particular change has put a strain on you. Be honest with yourself.

b. Now write down what you need. If you have a family and there is a particular activity that is feeling burdensome to you, perhaps you might need a break from it for a certain amount of time. Specify what it is you need, as well as the timeframe. If you need a holiday, that's ok too!

c. Finally, add the name of the people who might help you with each need and how they might be able to do so. Maybe your partner could help with a particular chore you have no time for, or your line manager could help you with time management at work.

d. Once you see the names of people who can help, consider if it seems more feasible to ask for that help. What would be the right time and place to ask for it? Think about how you might ask them, what the details of your request are (make it specific and be open as to why you need it and what the timeframe might be). Also think about how you might express your appreciation for their help.

Resources

Sandberg, Sheryl, & Grant, Adam – Option B: Facing Adversity, Building Resilience, and Finding Joy

Sullivan, Michele – Asking for help is a strength, not a weakness

45. Find new ways of connecting to your loved ones

"We all have battles to fight. And it's often in those battles that we are most alive: it's on the frontlines of our lives that we earn wisdom, create joy, forge friendships, discover happiness, find love, and do purposeful work." Eric Greitens

Loved ones, be they in or out of the family, are the people who help us stay strong in difficult times, and whom we feel we can rely on. In normal times, it is easy to forget to connect with them and perhaps take them for granted, but this often changes in time of need.

During difficult times such as the Covid-19 pandemic, you may have been forced apart from your loved ones. Many people have to self-isolate in separate homes or countries, and it is harder in general to connect to people in the way we used to. It is important therefore to nurture yourself in the ways you *can* connect, perhaps using the many technologies that are available today.

Activity

a. Think about the people in your immediate family, extended family and loved ones outside your family, which you haven't been in touch with recently, or not as much as you would have liked. Make a list of their names and contacts.

b. Choose the best medium to connect with them, or re-connect with them, so that they can easily receive your message. This could be in writing (text, email, and why not sending a card or letter like the old days), in audio (recorded message, phone call), or in video (video-recorded message, video-chat etc).

c. What would you like to communicate to them? Think about the things you might have taken for granted and that you can appreciate about them. Let them know that you love them, think about them and care for them. To some, this means extending a lifeline.

d. You never know the impact a warm word has on someone. Sometimes, it can go much further than you expected.

e. Do this unconditionally, without expecting anything in return. Sending these messages is really also a gift to you. What does it feel like once you've sent that message? Happy connecting!

Resources

Brown, Brené – Rising Strong

Brown, Brené – The Power of Vulnerability

46. Focus on how you can help someone else

"The best way to find yourself is to lose yourself in the service of others." *Mahatma Gandhi*

In times of difficulty, when perhaps we feel all out of control, let's look to see how we can help others. Yes, acknowledge your feelings of whatever is going on for you emotionally, financially, physically and psychologically, whilst at the same time considering how you might be an aid for others.

There are always volunteering opportunities to explore. Notice what you are interested in and consider how volunteering would be of help to others. The list is endless, here are a few ideas: support for families in crisis, shelter, soup kitchens, dog walking, helplines, animal rescue, food banks etc.

Activity

a. Make a list of initiatives you could consider getting involved with.

b. Research your top three, in terms of the skill set needed and the process for getting involved in the activities.

c. You can decide whether to move forward with choosing one of those activities identified in b. above.

Resources

Samuel, Julie – This Too Shall Pass: Stories of Change, Crisis And Hopeful Beginnings

Winfrey, Oprah – Oprah Gives A Masterclass On Manifestation And Vision Boards

47. Ask trusted friends for their views

"Each friend represents a world in us, a world possibly not born until they arrive, and it is only by this meeting that a new world is born." Anais Nin

Trusted friends are a great anchor in life. They are there when you need them and they are people you can trust to be candid with you. They are people who will listen and who will help.

It is great to be able to consult trusted people when you need to gain perspective on something and when you want to receive honest feedback (note that it is up to you what feedback and perspectives to take on board). Let's look at both.

Activity

a. If there is something that is worrying you, make time to speak to 2 or 3 trusted people about it, and be open to hear their perspective. Do they see things differently? What are you taking away that is helpful to you?

b. If you feel like you would like some support from them, ask them for it. This way you can weather the storm together. You're not alone!

c. Let's say you would like to receive honest feedback. First of all, choose the right person for this: not just someone you trust, but also someone who is able to give you the feedback you want. For example, if you are preparing a presentation for a meeting, you might want to look for a trusted colleague to act as the audience, or for a mentor who is experienced in giving presentations and can notice things that others wouldn't. Pick someone who will be straightforward with you, so that it will be helpful.

d. Remind them of the valuable aspects of feedback. Feedback needs to be specific and factual. It needs to address what you were saying or doing specifically – your verbal and non-verbal behaviours – and what impact that had. If you are taking feedback on board, brainstorm possible things you might do differently next time to improve your performance.

Resources

Covey, Stephen – The Speed of Trust: The One Thing that Changes Everything

Chase, Claire – Resilience Thinking for a Fractured World

48. Reach out to someone (or an organisation) to let them know how you're feeling

"No one is useless in this world who lightens the burden of another." Charles Dickens

You are not alone, even if sometimes it might feel that way. Are there people who you've lost contact with, that you would like to reconnect with? Think about people in different aspects of your life: family, friends, community, place of worship etc. who you could tap into and make contact with.

If no individuals come to mind, think about organisations that you could contact in order to break the isolation.

Activity

Make contact with someone in the next 24 hours to help break the isolation. Perhaps consider volunteering as a way to step outside of yourself.

Resources

Bridge, Frankie – Open: Why Asking For Help Can Save Your Life

The Orchard Enterprises – Lighten The Burden For Serenity And Inner Peace

49. Say 'yes' to help

"The moment you say yes to acting on your desire is the real beginning." Danielle LaPorte

Time to put down the mantle of being a superwoman or superman. This doesn't always serve you and can lead to stress and burnout. Give yourself permission to say 'yes' to offers of help and 'yes' to asking for help. It makes you stronger when you ask for and accept help. We are all like elastic bands - there is a fine line between our stretch and breaking points.

Activity

a. Think about aspects of your life you might need help with.

b. Consider who or what can help you. Consider too if this might be paid help or an exchange of favours with family/friends.

Resources

Townsend, John and Cloud, Henry – Boundaries, When To Say Yes, How To Say No To Take Control Of Your Life

Cohen, Lauren – How I Learned To Say Yes To Myself And Ask For Help

50. Maintain a tight circle of friends

"She is ... the mother I never had. She is ... the sister everybody would want. She is the friend that everybody deserves. I don't know a better person. I don't know a better person." Oprah Winfrey on her friendship with Gayle King

This can be so invaluable. These are the people you can go to and say anything to. These are the people who know the deepest part of you. These are the people that may be the bridge for you between sanity and insanity. These are the people you can go to and just cry, and go to a place beyond words.

Activity

a. Let your dearest friends know how much they mean to you.

b. In a circle of friends, write your name on the top of a sheet of A4 paper. Pass this to your friend on the left. That friend will write down (starting at the bottom of the page) one thing they appreciate about the person whose name is at the top of the page. Fold over the sheet of paper from the bottom to just cover the appreciation. Now pass this sheet of paper to the left and repeat until everyone has written an appreciation and you receive your paper back.

c. Continue this activity until each person ends up with their own sheet of appreciations, now everyone can take a read and share the appreciations as they wish.

Resources

Nelson, Shasta and Bentley, Amy Melissa – Friendships Don't Just Happen: The Guide To Creating A Meaningful Circle Of Girlfriends

Nelson, Shasta – Frientimacy: The 3 Requirements of All Healthy Friendships

51. Remain empathic

"Never look down on anybody unless you're helping him (them) up." Jesse Jackson

Empathy is: "Showing an ability to understand and share the feelings of another."

This demonstrates a level of resilience as you are then able to help others through hard times. Whilst you are showing compassion to others, you could remind yourself to show compassion to yourself too. This will help you on our journey through life.

Activity

a. Identify how you could be more empathic to others.

b. Notice when you could be more empathic to yourself.

Resources

Covey, Stephen – The 7 Habits Of Highly Effective People

Dunn, Elizabeth – Helping Others Makes Us Happy

52. Give your co-workers motivational feedback

"Things do not change; we change." Henry David Thoreau

Feedback is often considered criticism: you may have seen people become anxious at the prospect of receiving feedback from their boss! This is a huge shame, because feedback is meant to be helpful and given from a place of support, whether it is for improvement or to acknowledge something well done.

Often times, the feedback exchanged between people, especially at work, is the so-called "negative" feedback, which really ought to be called "developmental", as its aim is to help the person improve and grow. However, many miss out of the great opportunity to provide the so-called "positive" feedback, which ought to be called "motivational", because it is a great tool for self-awareness, best practice and motivation. This is the one you will be focusing on here.

Activity

a. Think about 5 to 10 people, both co-workers and others, whom you would like to give some motivational feedback.

b. Next to each name, write down the feedback you would like to give, pertaining to something you noticed that they did particularly well. Be very specific and describe:

1. the situation in which you observed them;

2. what specific behaviour you observed (verbal and/or non-verbal);

3. what impact it had on you or others (the business, etc);

4. if it applies, how this kind of behaviour is great to keep doing as a best practice.

c. Decide when, where and how you are going to deliver this feedback. Choose the appropriate time (sooner rather than later!), place and modality or medium. Face-to-face is a great way to deliver feedback, however if that is not possible, think about how the person might like to receive it (video of you, hand-written letter, etc). Make it detailed and personalised.

d. This is a great way for you to hone your skills in giving feedback too. What did you learn from this exercise?

Resources

Pink, Daniel – Drive: The Surprising Truth about What Motivates Us

MindTools – 5 Ways to Build Great Work Relationships

53. Tell your loved ones what you appreciate about them

"The most precious gift we can offer others is our presence. When mindfulness embraces those we love, they will bloom like flowers." Thich Nhat Hanh

Can you think of a movie in which the main character didn't tell their loved ones how much they meant to them until it was too late? This can also happen in real life, and sometimes we take our loved ones for granted.

It is a great gift to yourself when you share with others what you appreciate about them, be they loved ones or trusted friends or colleagues. Make sure you give specific feedback if you can, so that they too know what is great about them.

Activity

a. Think about 5 to 10 people you would like to show your appreciation to and write down their names.

b. Decide how you are going to show your appreciation. Is it going to be in person, on the phone, by letter or some other way? Think about how they would most like to receive it.

c. Decide when and where you're going to show your appreciation. Make it soon: tomorrow, this week, this month – not next year! Set a timescale for yourself to get it done.

d. Now think about what you are going to say. Tell them why you appreciate them and what exactly you appreciate about them. Is it something they did or displayed? What is that, when/where/how did they do it and how did it impact you or others positively? Be specific!

e. Ready, steady, go! Enjoy sharing your appreciation and also notice how it makes *you* feel when you do it.

Resources

Stavros, Jackie, & Torres, Cher, & Cooperrider, David – Conversations Worth Having: Using Appreciative Inquiry to Fuel Productive and Meaningful Engagement

Anderson, Joel – The Power of Presence

54. Build relationships that sustain you

"Relationships are built on trust. Without it, they wither and die." Brett & Kate McKay

Not all relationships will be sustaining. Some relationships devour you; others sustain you. Take a look at those relationships that help or hinder you and make some decisions about those.

Activity

a. Consider what you really value in relationships and make a list. You might value honesty, reliability and kindness.

b. Take a look at who in your relationships you get these things from, as well as look at whom you give these things to in your relationships.

Resources

Brody, Michelle – Stop the Fight! How To Break Free From The 12 Most Common Arguments And Build A Relationship That Lasts

Ogunjinmi, Femi – How To Tell If Someone Really Loves You

Mindfulness & Listening

55. Practice mindful living

"With mindfulness, you can establish yourself in the present in order to touch the wonders of life that are available in that moment." Thich Nhat Hanh

Mindfulness is often associated with a guru-like figure with crossed legs in a spiritual position on a mountaintop. However, mindfulness need not be just about hardcore long-hours meditation techniques. It is really about the attention you put on things on a daily basis.

Where your attention goes is your choice, so you can choose to set it on something in particular, and to make it stay there without distraction. Mindfulness is about putting 100% of your attention on one thing, rather than being distracted by multiple things, and being able to experience its depths.

Activity

a. Mindfulness can be related to something as simple as breathing. Set aside 5 minutes of your time (you can set a timer on your phone) to sit somewhere quiet, close your eyes, and focus on your breathing. While you are breathing, simply focus on where the air goes when you inhale it and exhale it. Feel your belly expand when you breathe in. Prolong your exhale so to empty your lungs completely, before your next breath. If your thoughts are going on a tangent, acknowledge your thoughts and let them go, then gently bring your attention back to your breathing. Once your time is over, check in with yourself: how does your body feel? When might you benefit from this type of mindfulness exercise? If it is helpful, set aside time for this in your diary, or take a break when you need it. Even a few minutes can help you find your centre again.

b. Mindfulness can be related to a task or an activity. Pick a task or activity, at work or outside of work (e.g. gardening, baking, finishing a piece of work). Set aside a time in which you know you will concentrate fully on that task (for example 20 minutes, 40 minutes or 1 hour). Commit yourself to this activity and nothing else. Make sure you eliminate all distractions and can communicate to others that you are unavailable during this time. Make sure you have anything you need: water and anything else you may need during the activity. Now that you are completely focused, go! Your attention will make you more productive and you will be able to immerse yourself more deeply in what you are doing, often with surprising and gratifying results.

c. Mindfulness can be applied to an aspiration. Ask yourself: "What is my aspiration?" After 10 seconds of reflection, write down your thoughts as they flow, without thinking too much. Define your aspiration and what practices can help you move towards it. Set those as the intention for your actions and the way you relate to the people around you. See what happens next!

Resources

Williams, Mark, & Penman, Danny – Mindfulness: The Eight-Week Meditation Programme for a Frantic World

Chow Trammel, Regina – Using Mindfulness to Deal with Everyday Pressures

56. Sit still

"Everything that's created comes out of silence. Your thoughts emerge from the nothingness of silence. Your words come out of this void. Your very essence emerged from emptiness. All creativity requires some stillness." Wayne Dyer

When all else fails, sit still.
When you don't know what else to do, sit still.
When you are in a state of confusion, sit still.
When you don't know what to think and feel, sit still.
When you are at a crossroads, sit still.
When you are pulled in all directions, sit still.
When you don't know what decision to make sit still.

In a place of silence, the answer often comes. See about allowing your mind to be still. There are so many ways to do this: being out in nature – sitting by a stream and listening to the rippling of the water, sitting in the garden, walking in some of our great parks and looking out at wonderful trees. Sitting in silence and closing your eyes, noting any thoughts that come in and allowing them to go out...

Activity

At least once a week, choose a time and place where you'll sit in silence.

Resources

Tolle, Eckhart – Stillness Speaks

Holiday, Ryan – How To Use Stillness To Achieve Greatness

57. Listen to your inner sounds

"Observe the space between your thoughts, then observe the observer." Hamilton Boudreaux

Being present means being aware first and foremost of yourself, starting from your body sensations and the sound of your breath.

The body holds immense wisdom, and all too often is not listened to. By listening to your body, you are able to notice how you are really feeling before the aches and pains make it apparent. You are also able to dive into the present moment and experience the *practice* of self-awareness.

Activity

a. Find a quiet place, indoors or outdoors, in a pleasant environment where you can relax.

b. Sit comfortably on a chair or cross-legged. If you are sitting on a chair, make sure both your feet are touching the ground. Keep your back straight but comfortable, not rigid, and imagine a string pulling your head gently towards the ceiling. Place your hands on your lap in a position that is symmetrical and feels comfortable to you.

c. Close your eyes, or, if you don't feel comfortable closing them, pick an unfocused point in the distance to lay your eyes on.

d. Focus on your breath. As you breathe in and out, follow the path of your breath and really hear the sounds it makes as you inhale, hold, and exhale. Repeat this 10 times, slowing down your breathing, and keeping your focus on the sounds of your breath.

e. Move your focus to your belly now, and feel your belly. Is it tight, is it heavy, is it light, is it grumbling? Are there any noises coming out from your belly? Internally, what does your belly sound like? Pick up the movements and sensations in your belly.

f. Slowly move down your body, stopping in different parts and listening to them. Are they making sounds? What are they telling you? If they could speak, what would they say? What do they need?

g. Just before moving to the next part of your body, re-centre yourself in your breath. Notice if the breath has changed, and what it sounds like. Dive deep into your breath, and let it guide you through your body.

h. When you experience thoughts that distract you from your listening, gently acknowledge them, let them go, and bring your focus back to where you want it to be. It's ok and normal to have thoughts, and it is your choice (and a useful practice) to re-focus.

i. When you have covered your body, return to your breath one more time. Slowly breathe in and out 5 times, with deep awareness of your breath, and gently open your eyes.

j. Note down for yourself what you noticed. What did your body have to say to you? What else comes to mind? Think about how you could use this information to improve your day.

Resources

Halliwell, Ed – Mindfulness: How to Live Well by Paying Attention

Herdieckerhoff, Elena – The gentle power of highly sensitive people

58. Use the power of attention

"Wings are not only for birds; they are also for minds. Human potential stops at some point somewhere beyond infinity." Toller Cranston

It is so easy to get distracted and unfocused in our daily lives, however we have a great gift that we can use: directing our attention where we want it to be. This can be a powerful tool for concentration, and it is also a mindful practice.

When you consciously choose where to focus your attention, it means that you are being present, here and now, with the activity or person you are with – including with yourself – and you are using your senses. Let's practice.

Activity

a. Pick a small fruit, like a berry, or a dried fruit like a sultana.

b. First of all, focus your attention on its shape and form. What do you notice about it? Have you ever looked at it so closely?

c. Feel its texture. Weigh it in your hand. Get a sense of what it feels like to touch it.

d. Now bring it close to your nose and smell it. What does it smell like? What does it remind you of? Does it make you feel drooly? Perhaps you now have a craving and would like to eat it.

e. If your mind starts going on a tangent, gently remind yourself to bring it back to your fruit and to *really* experiencing it to the fullest.

f. Bring it close to your lips and take a small bite, but don't swallow right away! Keep the piece of fruit in your mouth, roll it over in your tongue. What does it taste like? Feel your taste buds being stimulated by the fruit.

g. Slowly chew the fruit. Does it make a particular sound?

h. Place your attention on the taste: does the taste change as you chew it? How is it different from the taste of your first bite?

i. Finally, swallow the fruit and feel it going down your throat and towards your stomach.

j. Repeat with the next bit of fruit until you have consumed all of it.

k. What has this unusual experience of putting your whole attention on the process of tasting and eating taught you?

l. Have a think: where else in your life / work could you benefit from practicing a more mindful and focused attention? Write it down.

m. Once you have identified these areas, think about how you might do it. Do you need to slow down, make time, change something, in order to be able to increase your level of attention? Notice what providing more attention on those areas will achieve for you and how it will make a difference in your life.

Resources

Eyal, Nir, & Li, Julie – Indistractable: How to Control Your Attention and Choose Your Life

Chase, Sam – Paying Attention & Mindfulness

59. Listen to music

"Without music, life would be a mistake." Friedrich Nietzsche

Music helps to feed the soul. Music is great for any and every situation. Whatever music you like to listen to, do it often. It changes any given situation. It transports you to a different place. An opportunity to escape for a moment and be replenished to face the world.

Activity

a. How about putting together a playlist via whatever medium you choose, with music that you absolutely love and makes your heart sing.

b. Tap into your playlist and listen whenever you choose.

c. Keep it fresh by adding and deleting music of your choice.

Resources

Campbell, Don – The Mozart Effect: Tapping The Power Of Music To Heal The Body, Strengthen the Mind, and Unlock The Creative Spirit

Better Than Yesterday – How Music Benefits The Brain

60. Pause

"Between stimulus and response there is a space. In that space is our power to choose our response. In our response lies our growth and our freedom." Victor Frankl

Have you ever been in a situation where you took an impulsive action and then regretted it? It could be an email sent too quickly, or the wrong words coming out of your mouth and having an impact on someone else. Either way, reacting too quickly was the likely culprit.

A good way to control your impulses and make better decisions in the moment is to allow yourself to pause. Pausing is a great ally! It allows you to *respond* to a situation rather than *react* to it, and it gives you enough time to choose the best course of outcome in a given situation – or even to ask for more time if you require it. Sales techniques will often try to push buyers into committing right away, and appeal to their emotions. Pausing might be just the way to really think about what you're doing, and use your head more than your emotions to make that decision.

Activity

a. Think about the last few times you reacted to something or someone quite quickly, and this led to an undesirable outcome.

b. Be specific with yourself: what happened right before you took the impulsive actions? What were your thoughts and emotions in that moment?

c. If you were to go back and take a pause and a breath before that action, allowing you more time to think about your best course of action, what different actions could that have led to? What different outcomes?

d. In conclusion, what can a pause help you with in the future and what kind of time would you need? How will you notice when you need it and remind yourself to take a pause?

e. Now you can start practicing! Notice the change in behaviour and outcomes, and note them down on a journal to keep track.

Resources

The Dalai Lama, & Cutler, Howard – The Art of Happiness: A Handbook for Living

Gomez, Monique – Power of the Pause

61. Nurture your emotional needs

"The better you become at being able to recognize, verbalize, and manage your feelings, the less you will be vulnerable to losing emotional control or developing cardiovascular illnesses." Al Siebert

For some reason, it is not easy to think and communicate to ourselves and others about our emotions. However, one of the greatest things we can develop is our emotional intelligence.

Emotional intelligence starts from self-awareness, which leads to an improved ability to regulate our emotions, and leads to an improved ability to pick up and manage emotional situations around us.

So, what is it that you need that makes you feel happy, accomplished, safe or you-name-it?

Activity

a. Pick pen and paper and find a quiet spot where you will have time to think and write without interruptions.

b. Note down how you're feeling today. Use specific words: don't write words like "good" or "well", instead use words that are descriptive of your emotions. Are you irritated or enraged, joyful or content, or something in between?

c. What are 5 things you need today that will help you nurture your emotional needs?

d. Think about whether these things involve other people or not. What do you notice?

e. It is easy to rely on others for our happiness, but each of us is ultimately responsible for their own emotional state. If you wrote something like "I need X person to do Y thing for me", change it to something you can do *yourself* that will help you nurture your emotional needs. If you wrote "I need praise or recognition", fair enough, but why not start with yourself? What are the things *you* can praise and recognise about yourself?

f. What have you learned from this exercise?

Resources

Goleman, Daniel – Emotional Intelligence

David, Susan – The Gift and Power of Emotional Courage

62. Practice deep focus on a task

"Give your attention to the experience of seeing rather than to the object seen and you will find yourself everywhere." Rupert Spira

Though we live in a time of multi-tasking, doing more than one thing at a time is draining for the brain, as you are starting and stopping one thing to be interrupted by the next thing, and so on. Sound familiar?

What is nourishing for our brain is to focus on one thing – or a chunk of similar tasks – at a time. Have you experienced being really productive in a short span of time when you were able to really focus on what you were doing? Focus tweaks time your favour!

Activity

a. Make a list of the tasks you need to do on a particular day (it could be today or another day), preferably in advance of the day so you have time to plan and prepare.

b. Which tasks go well together? Group them by umbrella terms, for example: phone calls; project design; assessments and so on.

c. Depending on your schedule, are you able to group some of the similar tasks together, without distractions? For example: get all the phone calls done between 10-12?

d. There might be things that are already in your schedule, such as meetings, so make sure your different chunks work around those meeting times.

e. You might also want to give yourself some buffer zones – extra time that you can dedicate to unexpected issues or to things that take longer to complete.

e. If you don't want others to interrupt you, think about ways that you could let them know when you are available and when you are not. Is there a chunk of time you can dedicate to being available to others?

f. Ultimately, it is up to you to be assertive and say "no" when you can't meet other people's needs, especially if it is very disruptive for your work. Write down what you might need to say no to and how you are going to say it: polite but firm.

g. Don't forget to take breaks in between your "chunks". Without them, you can't sustain being productive. Plan for your breaks, including time for snacks, exercise, pauses, meals and taking a walk. Try to eat your meals away from your desk and focus on them separately than from work.

h. By increasing your focus on one thing at a time, you are likely to be more productive, more accurate and timelier. Give it a go and adjust your plan as you go to best suit your needs.

Resources

Tolle, Eckhart – The Power of Now

Bengtsson, Christina – The art of focus – a crucial ability

63. Get some well-deserved 'me' time

"Courage doesn't always roar. Sometimes courage is the quiet voice at the end of the day saying, "I will try again tomorrow." Mary Anne Radmacher

In a world that prides itself with "busy-ness", down time is often neglected and seen as laziness. 'Me' time, however, is really helpful to de-stress. It is time spent in the present moment, simply *being* rather than doing, doing, doing. If you are walking in the park, it means *just* doing that, for the sake of enjoying the park, *without* busying yourself thinking about the next deadline, and *without* distracting yourself with texting or phone calls. In fact, great 'me' time is time spent disconnected from technology, and reconnecting instead with yourself or the natural environment.

Sometimes 'me' time is a great way to crack a problem. If you've been obsessing with an issue that you haven't been able to solve, taking a break and doing something else – while your subconscious keeps working on it – often leads to an unexpected a-ha moment. Know the feeling?

Activity

a. Think about when you can plan some 'me' time in the day, week or month.

b. Where can you go for some 'me' time when you're at work? When you're at home? Or if you could travel somewhere, where would you go for some off-the-grid 'me' time?

c. Choose a spot and go there. Treat yourself to some joying doing nothing, just being.

d. Note down anything you noticed at the end of your 'me' time. How are you feeling now?

Resources

Covey, Stephen – First Things First

Puddicombe, Andy – All it Takes is 10 Mindful Minutes

64. Listen to the sounds of the environment

"The ability to observe without evaluating is the highest form of intelligence." Jiddu Krishnamurti

A great way to practice mindfulness is to focus your attention on external sounds. This has a calming effect on your senses, as you slow things down and take a moment to be present to what is around you.

Deep listening is a form of attentive listening that focuses your attention where you want to, in this case, on sounds. This means that while you listen, you strive to avoid distractions and you are choosing where to direct your focus.

Activity

a. Find a spot that inspires you, indoors or outdoors. If you can, go somewhere where you can be immersed in nature, such as a park.

b. Sit comfortably, feet touching the ground or cross-legged, and keep your back straight in a comfortable way, not rigid. Place your hands on your lap in a position that is symmetrical and feels comfortable to you.

c. Close your eyes, or, if you don't feel comfortable closing them, pick an unfocused point in the distance to lay your eyes on.

d. Focus on your breath first, to centre yourself. Follow the flow of your breath as you inhale, hold, and exhale.

e. As you keep on breathing, allow yourself to really listen to the sounds around you, be it a bird chirping in the distance, the sound of high heels, unintelligible chit-chat or the wind blowing.

f. What can you hear in the vicinity? Focus on it.

h. What can you hear in the distance? Focus there.

g. Let the sounds in, embrace them, be curious, and keep on breathing.

h. Then re-centre yourself in your breath, and slowly open your eyes. How are you feeling?

i. Note down for yourself what you noticed in the environment, and what you noticed in yourself.

Resources

Thich Nhat Hanh – The Miracle Of Mindfulness

Oliveros, Pauline – The difference between hearing and listening

65. Slow down

"Do not dwell in the past, do not dream of the future, concentrate the mind on the present moment." Buddha

In a rushed world, where fast-paced work environments are often celebrated, and busyness has almost become an obsession, it may feel unnatural and weird to slow things down. Before clocks and working days, dawn and dusk gave us the timings to wake up and go to sleep. Seasons and crops guided our diet and activities. Now, we have outsourced and commoditised things, and have forgotten what it means to slow down.

Think about what you are missing out on by doing things quickly and busying yourself with too many things at a time. When you slow down, you start noticing things more and at a different level. This is also true around awareness of physical and mental health. If you slow down, you are able to notice an illness before it becomes dire, you are able to see more clearly what you want and enjoy your experiences more deeply.

Activity

a. Pick a time to go out for a walk, with no other aim than to walk. You are not going anywhere and you don't have a deadline to arrive or go back.

b. Notice the speed and pace at which you are currently walking. And then slow it right down. Walk really, really slowly. How does it feel? Even if it feels strange, keep going and start noticing.

c. What do you notice as you walk more slowly? Internally, do you notice any particular thoughts? What is your emotional state right now? Externally, what do you see? Is there anything along the way that catches your eye? Anything that you hadn't noticed before? Take it all in.

d. Find a place where you can stop for a moment (a bench, a corner, a patch of grass) and breathe.

e. What did you learn from your experience of walking very, very slowly? What other areas and activities in your life could benefit from slowing down, both in personal and professional situations?

Resources

Sunim, Haemin – The Things You Can See Only When You Slow Down: How to be Calm in a Busy World

Chase, Sam – Paying Attention & Mindfulness

66. Meditate

"Meditation is like a gym in which you develop the powerful mental muscles of calm and insight." *Ajahn Brahm*

Meditation is the art of 'going within'. Collinsdictionary.com defines meditation as 'the act of remaining in a silent and calm state for a period of time, as part of a religious training, or so that you are more able to deal with the problems of everyday life'. Meditation is a pathway to peace and tranquillity. Done regularly, it can be used as a solutions-focused tool.

Meditation is a way to connect inwards to those areas that are most important to you. It's a place to go to be at one with yourself. There are any number of ways to get into a meditative state, for example, using a mantra (a very brief sentence) or counting backwards from a hundred noticing the numbers just float away, allowing them to drift off into the distance.

Activity

a. Find a time in your day where you won't be disturbed for 15 minutes. Sit on a chair or the floor in something comfortable, close your eyes.

b. Take a couple of deep, cleansing breaths. Breathe in for a count of 7, hold for a count of 5, breathe out for a count 7 and repeat five times.

c. From this peaceful place count backwards from a hundred allowing the numbers to just float away as you stay in meditation for 15 minutes.

d. Once out of meditation, spend a few moments noticing what you notice about your physiology, mindset and any points of resolution etc.

Resources

Harrison, Eric – Teach Yourself To Meditate: Over 20 Simple Exercises For Peace, Health and Clarity Of Mind

Mishler, Adriene – Meditation For Inner Peace

67. Turn to your inner world of faith and spirituality

"Remain open. There is something bigger." Iyana Vanzant

The extent to which you believe there is something bigger, beyond yourself that helps drive you, turn to your inner world of faith and spirituality. Spend a bunch of time there on a daily basis. Many answers reside there.

Activity

Consider something that you would like to resolve and spend some time in your inner world to understand what the answers may be. Some people sit in prayer, others in meditation, still others in simple silence. You might consider reading religious or spiritual books or listening to relevant podcasts that might aid you to turn inward to your world of faith and spirituality.

Resources

Tolle, Eckhart – The Power Of Now

Watts, Alan – A Crash Course On Spirituality

Goals & Mindset

68. When you fall down, pick yourself up

"If life knocks you down, try to land on your back. Because if you can look up, you can get up. And if you get up, you can stand up. And if you stand up, you can fight for your dream once again. You have something special. You have GREATNESS within you!" Les Brown

This really is at the heart of being resilient. Over the course of our lifetime, life offers many opportunities and difficulties. In those times when you are knocked sideways by life, or even knocked down all together, that's exactly the time to find a way to stand back up. It might take some time to brush yourself off and re-focus, what's important here though is your mindset. Your mindset is what helps you find a way to look over the horizon and see a path through to create for yourself.

Activity

a. Create a vision board of all the things you see on the horizon for yourself, so that when you fall, you'll have things to focus on that will help you to keep getting back up. Get as creative as you like using creative apps such as Canva (a graphic design platform that allows users to visual content). You could use PowerPoint, or cut out and stick pictures, write words, draw a vision of your future, etc.

b. Once you've completed your vision board:

I. Create a `Tree' diagram, starting with a major goal at the root of the tree.

II. Followed by major headings that we'll call the branches of the tree, these are major tasks that need to be completed in order to achieve your major goal.

III. Then identify the detailed steps needed to complete each task.

You'll then want to place these detailed steps in order of completion, as though they were the leaves on the branch.

Resources

Holiday, Ryan – The Obstacle Is The Way: The Art Of Turning Adversity To Advantage

Buxhoeveden, Stephanie – Thriving In The Face Of Adversity

69. Stand guard over your mindset

"Every day, stand guard at the door of your mind." Jim Rohn

When you read this, what are some of the first things that come to mind? To what extent do you believe you have control over your mind? Think about the thoughts that you think. The mind can be considered both a powerful and rich tool. It can also be easily manipulated. For a moment, don't think about a pink elephant. Don't let an image of a pink elephant come into your mind. Don't let that pink elephant meander around your thoughts. Did you think about the pink elephant? Did you let the image of the pink elephant come into your mind? Did you allow the pink elephant to meander around your thoughts?

I think the point has been made. The extent to which others are able to guide you into thinking thoughts you may or may not want to think are only matched by your choosing what thoughts you want to put into your head. It's a physical and psychological impossibility to hold two simultaneous thoughts in your head. That being the case, you can be consciously aware, and make decisions about what you think.

Activity

a. Sit quietly, on your own. Think about the thoughts that you would like to think. These will be thoughts that help to sustain you positively. Spend 10 to 15 minutes noticing the types of thoughts you would like to think more often.

b. At the end of your 10 to 15 minutes write out at least seven affirmations (creating a strong, positive, affirming statement about something as though it is already true e.g. 'my possibilities are vast'.

c. Spend 5 minutes a day saying these affirmations to yourself (out loud so that you can hear yourself) whilst looking at yourself in a mirror. Do this for 21 days.

d. In your journal, write down the positive changes that you notice about yourself, as well as about yourself in relation to your interactions with others.

Resources

Dweck, Carol – Mindset: How You Can Fulfil Your Potential

Crum, Alia – Change Your Mindset, Change The Game

70. Create your goals. Focus on them. Create a plan. Deliver.

"Everyone's dream can come true if you just stick to it and work hard." Serena Williams

What are your projected achievements over the next 6/9/12/18 months? Consider why these achievements are important to you. Who do you need to be, how do you need to think and how do you need to behave to turn those achievements into reality?

Discipline comes into this. Routine is also important. Being true to your word, and being honest with yourself will take you far. Consider how you might leverage aspects of what you want to achieve.

Activity

a. Consider what you want to achieve and why.

b. Put each goal in a timeframe. Take a look at your six-month goals and break them down into achievable activities over 6 months, 3 months, monthly and weekly. Schedule these in your diary.

Resources

Holder, Jackee – Be Your Own Best Life Coach: Take Charge And Live The Life You Always Wanted

Leggett, Amara – Develop A Plan: Make The Impossible Possible

71. Change your thinking. If one thing doesn't work, try something else.

"Progress is impossible without change, and those who cannot change their minds cannot change anything." George Bernard Shaw

There are times when we need to do things differently and to do different things. This is an act of creativity, where you recognise that some things aren't working and it's time to do something else.

Activity

Consider something you need new thinking about. Then consider the situation from different points of view, as suggested below.

I. In first position (your point of view), note down your understanding of the situation.

II. In second position (perhaps a trusted friend's point of view), consider what they might do to remedy the situation.

III. In third position (an external observer's point of view) how might they remedy the situation?

Resources

Gillihan, Seth J – Retrain Your Brain: Cognitive Behavioural Therapy In ix Weeks

Bilyeu, Tom – In Order To Change Your Life, you need to learn this first!

72. Stay razor focused on your goals, particularly when there is a pull to do otherwise

"Focus on the possibilities for success, not on the potential for failure." Napoleon Hill

Daily focus on your goals will bring you what you want. Even when there is limited time in the day to focus, even carving out five-minute time slots throughout the day will help to ensure you're on your path towards your achievements.

Activity

a. Identify how many five-minute time slots you can find in one day. Perhaps start off with two five-minute time slots in a day, over 7 days: that's seventy minutes in a week, two hundred and eighty minutes every four weeks in a year, that's three thousand, six hundred and forty minutes in total. Before you know it, you'll be ticking off your goal achievements.

b. Note down what goals you will achieve incrementally using this method.

Resources

Nichols, Lisa – No Matter What: 9 Steps To Living The Life You Love

Pinero, Eddie – Limitless Possibilities

73. Create your personal mission statement

"Make your life a mission – not an intermission." *Arnold H. Glasgow*

This helps you understand what your purpose in life is. It helps you understand your reason for being. This focuses you on what you want to say 'yes' to and leave the rest to others. It helps to align who you are and what you do in the completion of your goals.

Treat your mission statement as a motto that helps to guide your life. Your personal mission statement, according to Stephen Covey, is about "defining the personal, moral and ethical guidelines within which you can most happily express and fulfil yourself."

Some examples of personal mission statements are:

"Not merely to survive, but to thrive; and to do so with some passion, some compassion, some humour and some style". Maya Angelou

"I want to serve the people. And I want every girl, every child to be educated." Malala Youafzai

"To have fun in my journey through life and learn from my mistakes." Richard Branson

Activity

Create a personal mission statement by focusing on the following key elements: your personality, your values, what interests you, what you are passionate about, your skills, strengths, knowledge and talents. Be sure to keep your mission statement to one or two sentences, as in the examples above. This may take a number of attempts. Stay with it, that is a part of the process.

Resources

Covey, Stephen – How To Develop Your Mission Statement

Anderson, David – Why Am I Here? Discover Your Personal and Professional Mission#

74. Become a bouncy ball, giving yourself no other choice than to seek another mindset

"I hated every minute of training, but I said, 'Don't quit. Suffer now and live the rest of your life as a champion." Muhammad Ali

Your mindset is remarkable. Minute to minute you can decide how you respond to a given situation.

"A bouncy ball or rubber ball is a spherical toy ball, usually fairly small, made of elastic material which allows it to bounce against hard surfaces. When thrown against a hard surface, bouncy balls retain their momentum and much of their kinetic energy (or, if dropped, convert much of their potential energy to kinetic energy). They can thus rebound with an appreciable fraction of their original force." Wikipedia

Activity

When you read the above, notice what your visceral response is, make notes in your journal. Focus more here on your feelings rather than your thinking responses. To what extent do you bounce back from difficult situations? What strategies do you use to bounce back? How does your ability to bounce back drive how you operate in the world, particularly in terms of how you might adapt your mindset to a range of life situations?

Resources

Newmark, Amy – Chicken Soup For The Soul: Step Outside Your Comfort Zone

Thomas, Eric – How The Mind Works

75. Never give up. Always look for a way to achieve your result areas

"Nothing in the world can replace perseverance. Talent will not; nothing is more common than unsuccessful people with talent. Genius will not; unrewarded genius is almost legendary. Education will not; the world is full of educated derelicts. Perseverance and determination alone are omnipotent." Calvin Coolidge

What could possibly get in your way? Or put it another way, what would ensure that you continue to achieve your results?

Activity

a. Consider who or what in your life is taking your energy in a negative way.

b. Brainstorm what you need to do in order to overcome the above.

Resources

Meyer, Joyce – Never Give Up!: Relentless Determination to Overcome Life's Challenges

Scott, Ben Lionel – Never Give Up

76. Ensure you have an open mindset

"The mind is just like a muscle, the more you exercise it, the stronger it gets and the more it can expand." Idowu Koyenikan

An open mindset is one where you consider life's opportunities. You consider life's possibilities. You consider challenges as a fork in the road to make sometimes quite difficult decisions. You understand the importance of your own efforts and attitude in determining your own abilities.

You recognise that you are not the font of all knowledge and that you are open to taking on board constructive feedback. You draw inspiration from the success of others and are open to doing new things.

Activity

Make a list of ways in which you demonstrate an open mindset.

Resources

Alderton, Jamie – Proven Strategies To Build Up Your Brain, Body and Business

Dweck, Carol – The Power Of Believing You Can Improve

77. Plan just today

"The time to repair the roof is when the sun is shining." John Fitzgerald Kennedy

Sometimes it's hard to look beyond today and one day at a time feels like that is all you can do. Ok, well do just that. Plan what your today looks like.

Activity

a. Break your day down into one and a half-hour manageable chunks and decide what you are going to do in each of those chunks of the day.

b. Remember to build in your breaks throughout the day too.

Resources

Chatterjee, Rangee – The 4 Pillar Plan: How To Relax, Eat, Move And Sleep Your Way To A Longer, Healthier Life

Dispenza, Joe – Unlock The Full Potential Of Your Mind

78. If planning today feels like too much, just plan the next hour

"Every minute you spend in planning saves 10 minutes in execution; this gives you a 1,000 percent return on energy!"
Brian Tracy

Only focus on having yourself occupied for four 1-hour slots in the day. That's all, no more. If that feels like it's too much, just plan for one 1-hour time slot in the day. Your actions will soon add up.

Activity

Plan your 'to-do activities' to be completed in one-hour time chunks (be sure to have a break after one hour.

Resources

Hardy, Darren – The Compound Effect: Multiply Your Success One Simple Step At A Time

Cartoon Studio – One Step At A Time

79. Create a vision of where you want to be in 2, 5, 10 years

"Whatever you can do or dream you can, begin it. Boldness has genius, and magic and power in it. Begin it now." Johann Wolfgang von Goethe

Why is this important? If you don't have a dream, a vision of where you want to go or where you want to end up, you could end up anywhere.

Activity

a. Assess your current situation. Are you where you want to be?

b. Note down what you are happy with and what you want to change.

c. Decide on a timeframe of what you want to do and where you want to be in some aspect of your life, be it personal, financial, career, health etc.

d. Take yourself to that place, let's say in 2 years. Create a vivid representation of who you are and what you are doing. Create this in minute detail (write in the present tense as if your situation were true and real for you).

e. From that place of 2 years from now (as if in the present time, looking back to two years prior), note down what you did to achieve who and where you are. Write down in minute detail all the steps you took to achieve it. (There you have your plan of action for the next two years).

Resources

Gawain, Shakti – Creative Visualisation

Morrissey, Mary – The Power Of Writing Down Your Dreams And Goals

Wellness & Self-Care

80. Exercise physically

"Take care of your body. It's the only place you have to live."
Jim Rohn

Taking care of your body is part of the resilience toolkit. It is actually something that enhances your neuroplasticity. What this means is that physical exercise helps your brain grow connections between neurons, your brain cells.

Physical activity can also improve your memory, and it helps you produce some feel-good chemicals. If you're not the gym type, engaging in some type of aerobic exercise every day, such as walking for example, is a good way to help your body. Aerobic exercises involve increasing your breathing and heart rate in a sustained way, and can be done at home.

Some examples of aerobic exercises are: walking, swimming, jogging / running, cycling and rope jumping. Other examples include Zumba, using the elliptical machine at the gym, gym-cycling and cardio kickboxing. There are also various apps you can choose from which will help you make a plan for yourself and keep yourself accountable. Regularity is of the essence.

Activity

a. Choose one or more activities that you like doing and you know will be likely able to commit to in your current circumstances. If the pool is far away and you don't have time to drive there, shower etcetera, don't choose swimming. The more enjoyable the activity, the more likely you will be to stick to it.

b. Make space for aerobic exercise in your diary, possibly every day for at least 30 minutes. Include when and where the exercise will take place and how you will organise it in your day. Decide how you can help yourself stick to your plan.

c. Use your journal to make a note of what you noticed. Did you find it easy or difficult on a particular day? Did you notice any changes / progress after a week or a month?

d. If you want to keep track of interesting vital signs such as your breathing and heart pace, consider getting yourself a health and fitness tracker – usually in the form of a bracelet – which can track your vitals and help you become more aware of the effects of exercise on your body.

Resources

St. John, Bonnie – Micro-Resilience: Minor Shifts for Major Boosts in Focus, Drive, and Energy

Suzuki, Wendy – The brain-changing benefits of exercise

81. Get into a routine

"Chains of habit are too light to be felt until they are too heavy to be broken." Warren Buffet

Routine helps towards being disciplined. Discipline brings you your rewards. Whatever those rewards might be, you're more likely to be effective having a disciplined routine in place. It might be that, in order to allow for some flexibility and deal with the 'unknowns', you routinise at least 60% of your day.

Activity

Take a look at your daily and weekly patterns and decide if there's anything you can focus on to make it more of a routine, e.g. bed time, wake time, workout time, etc.

Resources

Glei, Jocelyn – Manage Your Day To Day, Build Your Routine, Find Your Focus And Sharpen Your Creative Mind

Smith, Will – Self Discipline (best motivational videos)

82. Give yourself pampering treats on a regular basis

"It's not selfish to love yourself, take care of yourself, and to make your happiness a priority. It's necessary." Mandy Hals

Pamper pamper pamper. Just wanted to say that three times. There are occasions when you might forget to pamper yourself, particularly as women (with the competing demands of everyday life both within and outside the home) and put yourself at the centre of your universe. It's so important to do this. Why? It provides you with the fuel to step out into the world to do and be the best you that you can be.

The pampering doesn't have to be something extravagant like a week or two on a pampering retreat. It could be something as simple as soaking your feet in warm water with lovely essential oils of your choosing. Or perhaps a deep soak in a bath with wonderfully scented bath salts (sea and/or Epsom salts).

Activity

a. Make a list of low-cost pampering activities you could do for yourself or with a group of friends.

b. Decide if you'd like to be part of or create a pampering circle of at least a group of four (probably best to keep it as an even number, so you can do pampering activities in pairs).

c. Schedule time for your pampering session.

Resources

King, Vex and Hay House UK – Good Vibes, Good Life: How Self Love Is The Key To Unlocking Your Greatness

Nyema, Gen Kelsang – Happiness Is All In The Mind

83. Dance and release

"The only way to make sense out of change is to plunge into it, move with it, and join the dance." Alan Watts

When we are stressed, there can be pent-up emotions and energy. This is common also in sedentary jobs that require long periods of sitting at a desk without moving. This is why movement is very healthy for our body and our brain, and it helps release stress and tensions, as well as activate feel-good chemicals.

Dancing in particular activates the brain's sensory and motor circuits. It develops musical and rhythmic intelligence, and it also increases neuroplasticity, which is the ability to create and reorganise synaptic connections.

Activity

a. Do you prefer dancing on your own, in the same space with others or in partnered dances? Make a list of dances you already engage in, and dances you would like to learn or experience. For example, you could try 5 Rhythms or contact dancing, or tango. Or maybe you just like to put the music on in your home and dance to particular rhythms.

b. If meeting other people is not possible, for example in the event of self-isolation, you can find online groups that meet on digital platforms (like Zoom and others) to dance together at parties or other events. Find out what is out there and make a list of what might interest you.

c. Make time for it: when will you dedicate time to dancing and releasing? Can you make it a regular thing? Make a commitment to yourself.

d. Buddy up with someone who will help you keep motivated and committed to regular dancing for your health and wellbeing. Enjoy!

Resources

Walsh, Mark – Embodiment - Moving beyond mindfulness

Bose, Brian – Dance your way to empowerment

84. Monitor your sleep patterns

"Sleep is our recharge function and our reset button...and we all need a reset button sometimes." Sam Owen

Resilience is not just about adaptability: it is also about self-care and healthy habits. Sleep is particularly important because it affects how we function. Without sleep, we tend to make bad decisions and mistakes, and our wellbeing rapidly deteriorates.

When we sleep, our body restores itself as well as our mind. Sleep is when memories and learnings from the day are consolidated, so that we can recall them. This affects focus, learning and behaviours. How regular is your sleep? What are your patterns? Monitoring your sleep, for example through wearing a fitness tracker, could give you an insight on how you sleep and help you become aware of what works or doesn't work for your wellbeing.

Activity

a. Have a think about the quality of your sleep. How would you rate it from 1 to 10 (1 being very low, and 10 being very high)? How many hours do you typically sleep? Do you have a regular sleep time? Does the amount of sleep vary?

b. Is there anything you would like to change about your sleep patterns? If so, what kind of behaviours do you need to change in order to sleep better? Note down your answers and pick one action to carry out in the next month. This could simply be a cut-off time to go to bed.

c. Monitor your sleep for 2 to 4 weeks. You can do this 'manually' by recording timings and how you feel during the day, for example. You could also get yourself a fitness tracker and learn about how much light, rem and deep sleep you get each night, how many times you get up and more data which is organised for you in graphs.

d. What have you noticed after 2-4 weeks of monitoring your sleep? Are you keeping up with your chosen action? If so, what has changed as a result of implementing that action?

e. What other things might you want to improve? With knowledge from your monitoring, list any other actions you would like to take to further improve your sleep patterns.

f. Repeat monitoring and actions until you are happy with the outcome.

Resources

Walker, Matthew, & Sackville, John – Why We Sleep: The New Science of Sleep and Dreams

Donovan, Jim – How To Trick Your Brain Into Falling Asleep

85. Eat well, eat healthy

"A few people are born resilient. The rest of us need to work consciously at developing our abilities." Al Siebert

Helping our body to cope includes nourishing it with a healthy diet. There are lots of different suggestions on what kind of diet is a good diet, but it also depends on your unique metabolism, your culture and your lifestyle.

Food adjustments are really lifestyle adjustments, which factor in how much exercise you have each day, whether your job includes movement and so on. There is no better advisor than yourself!

Activity

a. Over the next week, monitor yourself and your habits. Note down what food you eat at each meal, and when meals and snacks happen. If you want to be even more detailed, note down the calories for each food intake.

b. Also note down the exercise you have during the week: what it is, when it is, how long, and if you want to be detailed add how many calories burnt it amounts to.

c. At the end of the week, look back at your data. What do you notice? Is there anything you would like to change in order to be healthier?

d. If you have a healthy-eating goal, note down specifically what that is and make a plan to achieve it. For the next month, what are you going to do differently that will bring you closer to your goal? What is feasible: what can you make time for? How are you going to hold yourself accountable?

e. Time to carry out your plan. Keep monitoring and noting down the details for the next month and at the end of the month see what's changed and decide how you want to move forward.

f. Don't forget to celebrate your successes – if you are moving towards a healthier diet and lifestyle, you will reap the rewards!

Resources

Macchiochi, Jenna – Immunity

Robertson, Ruairi – Food for thought: How your belly controls your brain

86. Address your physical needs

"No matter how much falls on us, we keep ploughing ahead. That's the only way to keep the roads clear." Greg Kincaid

Don't wait for your body to ache! If you listen closely, your body will let you know if something is not right: all you need to do is listen. It will also let you know when it is happy – you will have the feel-good sensations.

Being aware of your physical sensations is helpful *before* things get bad. It is very useful to do some prevention rather than ignore the signs of illness or stress until later, when it might be much more difficult to recover. We have one body in life, so we had better take care of it!

Activity

a. Find a quiet space to sit down and close your eyes.

b. Take a few deep breaths and listen to your body. How is it feeling? Let your body tell you what is going on.

c. Breathe through your body from the tip of your head to the tip of your toes. Every time you inhale, focus on one part of the body. When you exhale, relax that part of your body. Then scan the rest of your body, starting from your head, face, neck and all the way down to your feet. Try to cover the whole of your body, and feel free to breathe longer into those areas where your body feels tense, so you can relax them.

d. When you are ready, bring yourself back to the room and reflect: what have you learned from this check-in? What has your body told you?

e. Now note down specifically what your physical needs are in this moment. Do you need to lie down and rest? Do you need to move and exercise? Do you need to eat? What does your body need?

f. What does your body need in the short, medium and longer term?

Resources

Meurisse, Thibaut – Master Your Focus: A Practical Guide to Stop Chasing the Next Thing and Focus on What Matters Until It's Done

Waterfall, Sam – Nurturing Your Inner Ecosystem

87. Sleep

It's really important to get enough sleep. So, what is enough sleep for adults? For most people, it is somewhere between seven and nine hours. It is difficult to function optimally without enough sleep. Are you an "early to bed, early to rise" or a "late to bed, late to rise" type of sleeper? Late to bed, early to rise, doesn't really work in the long term: it depletes your energy and immune system over time.

What if you can't sleep when you go to bed? There are lots of natural remedies out there to check out: essential oils (e.g. lavender, clary sage, sweet marjoram, bergamot. These can be used with a base oil to rub on your skin, placed in a humidifier or oil burner), teas (chamomile, valerian, lemongrass, peppermint), meditation, vitamin products that include melatonin etc.

Activity

a. Take a look at your best/favourite sleep pattern and ensure you're getting between 7 and 9 hours' sleep a night.

b. If you're challenged by getting enough sleep check out some of the natural remedies.

Resources

Walker, Matthew and Sackville, John – Why We Sleep: The New Science Of Sleep and Dreams

Rogan, Joe – The Science Of Sleep

88. Enjoy nature

"I have always been delighted at the prospect of a new day, a fresh try, one more start, with perhaps a bit of magic waiting somewhere behind the morning." John Boynton Priestley

Spending time in nature has a special soothing effect, and can help nurture both physical and mental health. Activities that can be done in nature, such as a park or forest, include exercising, planting trees, walking the dog and observing animals in their natural habitat.

A natural environment is good for the lungs and facilitates breathing, away from the pollution of cities and cars. It can also help shift moods, usually with a calming effect that helps to become aware of oneself and surroundings in a mindful way. How much time do you spend in nature?

Activity

a. Make a list of nature environments near your home, both at walking distance and further.

b. List all the different ways in which you can enjoy the natural environments you mentioned. What kind of animals might you observe there? What kind of activities could you do there? Perhaps jogging, sunbathing or swimming? You could even spend time just listening to birds, journaling or reading a book. Which places would you go to for some me-time and which ones would you invite others to? Think about how to enjoy these natural environments in a mindful way.

c. Make a list of the benefits you would reap from spending time in nature. Think about physical benefits, mental benefits, spiritual benefits, and anything else that comes to mind.

d. Check your diary and pick out a regular time in which you can visit those natural environments: for example, once a day or once a week.

e. Make a commitment to yourself and tell yourself why you want to make this a healthy habit. If it helps, find a buddy to share this commitment with and to help keep each other accountable.

Resources

The Mindfulness Project – Into Nature: Mindful ways to unplug and reconnect

Overton, Sara – How Mindfulness in Nature Can Transform Us & Climate Change

89. Laugh regularly

"If you laugh, you change, and if you change, the world changes around you." Madan Kataria

Laughing is a great way to keep yourself healthy and happy. Even when there is nothing to laugh about, it is still helpful to stimulate our laughter. We can do so either through our mind (jokes, comedies) or through our body.

Bringing our body to laugh is a great way to exercise, breathe and be playful. It also helps your brain produce endorphins and other chemicals which relax you and help you feel happier. This is the basis of a global practice called laughter yoga, which combines laughter and breathing as a form of exercise.

Some benefits of laughter include: reinforcing your immune system, regulating blood pressure and heart rate, breathing more deeply through your diaphragm, feeling more confident and joyful, bonding with others, changing your mood. There are laughter clubs all over the world that you can meet up in person and also online.

Activity

a. When you wake up in the morning, take a few deep breaths and then stimulate some laughter. If you are laying on your back, bring your knees towards your chest, lock them with your arms, gently rock yourself left and right, and while you do so allow yourself to giggle and outright laugh for the next 5 minutes. It might seem strange, but it might also get your day started on the right tone!

b. Whenever you want, you can apply your own laughter cream. Bring out your hand: the invisible laughter cream is always available in your hand. Pick some cream and apply it to your face. As soon as you apply it, it causes giggles.

c. You can also practice laughing and breathing with others. Sit in front of each other and look at each other in the eye – you can make silly faces too if you like but there is no talking. Take some deep breaths and then start laughing. You can stimulate the laughter but you don't need to force it, you can also listen and allow the laughter contagion to come to you!

d. It is easier to laugh in a group, so you can always join a laughter club. Google "laughter yoga" or "laughter club" and the name of your area. Look for teachers on laughteryoga.org or look them up on social media. You can also participate in online laughter taster sessions, via Skype and Zoom.

Resources

Kataria, Madan – Inner Spirit of Laughter- 5 Secrets from The Laughing Guru

the other song – TEDMED Live Talk by Dr. Madan Kataria at the other song

Learning & Motivation

90. Learn something new

"The significant problems we face cannot be solved at the same level of thinking we were at when we created them." Albert Einstein

As humans, we are constantly learning, both by mastering what we do, and by learning new things. Learning new things is a great workout for the brain, and can be an exciting and stimulating exercise.

It is often when learning something new that you are able to also learn something new about yourself, and surprise yourself with skills you didn't know you had. Socrates used to say: "I know that I know nothing" – a humbling attitude that highlights even more the need to keep learning.

Activity

a. Make a list of new things you would like to learn, be it learning another language, cooking a particular recipe or enhancing a professional skill.

b. What is exciting about each item of the list? Note it down.

c. How might learning these new things be helpful to you in the future? Note it down.

d. Choose the items you can fit in your diary and prioritise them by numbering them. Some may happen in parallel if you want to.

e. Now write down your learning action plan. What timescales are you going to commit for each chosen item? When and where will you focus on your learning?

f. Also think about how to keep yourself accountable. If you have to skip a “learning appointment”, what is your plan B? When are you going to make up for it?

g. Enjoy and happy learning!

Resources

David, Susan – Emotional Agility: Get Unstuck, Embrace Change and Thrive in Work and Life

Cahn, Lu Ann – Why We Must Do New Things to Live a Happier Life

91. Use empowering words

"Resilience isn't a single skill. It's a variety of skills and coping mechanisms. To bounce back from bumps in the road as well as failures, focus on emphasizing the positive." Jean Chatzky

When describing yourself and your endeavours to others, do you use powerful, confidence-inducing, exciting words, or do you tend to minimise your achievements and be super-humble?

Using empowering words can go a long way not only to "sell" your competencies to potential employers or your team, but also to boost your self-belief and confidence, increase your motivation and make you feel good too.

Activity

a. Pick a friend or colleague to practice introducing yourselves to each other in 2 minutes. The other person takes notes for feedback.

b. Give each other feedback. What impact did the introduction you heard have on you? Be honest about the impact and specific about what exactly your friend said and did that contributed to that impact. Notice each other's body language too.

c. Could you perhaps have given yourself more credit? If the answer is yes, spend the next 2 minutes choosing 2 or 3 achievements you want to highlight and be clear about why you are proud of them. Choose words that make you feel empowered, so that you give yourself the credit you deserve.

Tip: use "I" instead of "we" or "the team" to describe your personal contributions!

d. Introduce yourselves again and give each other feedback. What has changed? Look for changes in words and also in the way the words were said. Was the body language different? Was the impact different? What changed specifically?

e. Discuss together what verbal and non-verbal cues felt empowering to the speaker, and which ones had a powerful impact on the audience. Do they match? Are there things you feel like you could benefit from developing further?

f. Note down what you would like to practice more of and develop when you introduce yourself. For example, you might decide to take on board some of the feedback and make a plan to use more active verbs, be more concise and increase the volume when you speak.

Resources

Whitmore, John – Coaching for Performance: The Principles and Practice of Coaching and Leadership

Asante, Amma – The power of defining yourself

92. Listen to motivational podcasts

"Your comfort zone is a place where you keep yourself in a self-illusion and nothing can grow there but your potentiality can grow only when you can think and grow out of that zone." Rashedur Ryan Rahman

Staying motivated requires some form of positive action, it doesn't just happen. Listening to motivational podcasts, of which there are many, as you go about your day is empowering. These can set you up to move further forward. They can help to unstick you when you feel stuck. They are like a breath of fresh air when you need to clear the fog in your head.

Activity

Think about the types of information that help to motivate you and seek that out on your preferred podcast platform.

Resources

Peters, Steve – The Chimp Paradox: The Mind Management Programme To Help You Achieve Success

Be Inspired – "I Am" Affirmations For Success, Wealth and Happiness

93. Continually upskill yourself

"Learn as if you were not reaching your goal and as though you were scared of missing it." Confucius

There's always an opportunity to learn. Why wouldn't you though? Nothing stays the same. Change is the key constant in life. Without upskilling and changing, we atrophy.

Is there something that you have wanted to learn for some time, but haven't got around to for one reason or another? If so, what is it?

Activity

Have a conversation with a friend about a new skill you'd like to learn.

Do the research you need to do and get it done!

Resources

Soukup, Ruth – Do It Scared: Finding the Courage To Face Your Fears

Ferriss, Tim – Why You Should Define Your Fears Instead Of Your Goals

94. Use empowering poses

"Your mind and attitudes create either barriers or bridges to good outcomes." Al Siebert

Body and mind are deeply interconnected. Your mind influences your body. If you are worried, your body might feel heavy, or some parts might tense up. If you are happy, your body might feel lighter and your energy levels may be higher.

Similarly, your body influences your mind too. If you spent the next 10 minutes slouching, frowning and looking at the floor, your mood would rapidly go downhill. If you did something energising, your mind would feel energised too. If you adopted a powerful pose, you would probably feel confident and ready.

How your body and mind interact will be unique to you, and you can see for yourself if power poses are something you might benefit from and how.

Activity

a. Find a room with enough space and privacy to try out some poses.

b. Stand with a straight stance, eyes forward, chin up, shoulders back, feet grounded to the floor at shoulders' distance. How does it make you feel?

c. Now open your arms wide and bring them upwards so that you're wide open. Hold this position for 10 seconds. How does it make you feel?

d. Now bring your arms to your waist, maintaining a straight posture. Hold it. Do you feel more empowered?

Resources

Rosenberg, Joan – 90 Seconds to a Life You Love: How to Turn Difficult Feelings into Rock-Solid Confidence

Cuddy, Amy – Your body language may shape who you are

95. Read a life-affirming book

"I must say I find television very educational. The minute somebody turns it on, I go into the library and read a good book." Groucho Marx

It's good to read consistently. To deepen your mind, to deepen your understanding of the world. Your reading doesn't need to be earth shatteringly deep. Just read whatever you want to (some people do though have a preference for podcasts). Reading opens up our world to a range of possibilities.

Perhaps read recommendations from others. I like to do this because it means I'm stepping out of my `normal' and opening myself up to something I hadn't thought of before.

Activity

a. Read a book that's outside of your `normal'.

b. Perhaps join or start a book club to discuss some of your favourite books. This can either be done online, in person or a combination of the two.

Resources

Evaristo, Bernadine – Girl, Woman, Other

Bu, Lisa – How Books Can Open Your Mind

96. Listen to empowering music

"Like tiny seeds with potent power to push through tough ground and become mighty trees, we hold innate reserves of unimaginable strength. We are resilient." Catherine DeVrye

Music can affect mood and emotion very quickly. Soothing music can be relaxing and upbeat music can be an energy booster. This is because music can stimulate the release of dopamine, the neurotransmitter connected to our pleasure and reward centre in our brain.

When you want to boost your energy and your motivation, setting the right music for it can uplift you and it can also be fun! What is your favourite music pieces for your different moods?

Activity

a. Go through your music library, Spotify or your favourite digital music streaming service and choose an energy-boosting song.

b. As you listen to that song, become aware of the effects it has on your body. Do you feel like moving? Allow your body to follow the rhythm freely.

c. Now become aware of the effect the song is having on your mood and thoughts. How are you feeling now? What are you thinking about?

d. Try doing this before a difficult or heavy task, to get yourself revved up. Has your motivation increased?

e. Now make a playlist for your different moods, and keep adding to it as you hear songs that could go in the list. Different moods or emotions could include: happy, relaxing, energising, soothing, and so on.

f. If you want to keep track of the effects of different music types on your mood and actions, keep a journal on it. Happy listening!

Resources

Reynolds, Basil – Finding the Music Inside: Your inner algorithm to a more meaningful life!

Harvey, Alan – Your brain on music

97. Give your older self a message

"Be the change you wish to see in the world." *Mahatma Gandhi*

We don't know what the future holds for us, but the past becomes part of our present and our present part of our future. There is certainly wisdom in what you have experienced so far, and what your deep desires are for the future.

Wouldn't it be lovely to receive a letter from yourself, sometime down the line? This is a chance to be honest and creative, and write a message to yourself from now, that you can read in the future. Perhaps it will remind you of your dreams and how you would like to see the world.

Activity

a. Pick a quiet spot to sit and write on a letter or a card – something lovely that you would absolutely *love* to receive. Make sure you have at least 30 minutes to write without distractions – and if you need more time feel free to take your time!

b. Decide when you want your older self to open your letter, perhaps 1, 5 or 10 years from now. Pick a date: month and year. On the front of the envelope that you will use, write your name and the date that you have chosen to open it.

c. What would you like to say to your future self? Without thinking too much, start writing what comes to mind. Don't worry about grammar or punctuation, as long as it is legible to you.

d. Perhaps you might like to talk about your experiences and what you have learned: how will that help the future you?

e. Perhaps you would like to share your current dreams, and the life you would like to have, and the world you would like to live in in your future. What are your goals, passions and dreams?

f. When you have finished writing, put your letter in the envelope and seal it. Depending on the date you have set to re-open it, make sure it stays in a place where you will be able to find it in the future – whether you stay in the same home or you move. And when the time comes, let what you wrote inspire you.

Resources

Ginsberg, Phyllis – Brain Makeover: A Weekly Guide to a Happier, Healthier and More Abundant Life

Sears, JP – Saying YES! to your Weirdness

Reframing & Visualising

98. View challenges as opportunities

"When one door of happiness closes, another opens; but often we look so long at the closed door that we do not see the one which has been opened for us." Helen Keller

Resilience has a lot to do with your frame of mind, that is, literally how you choose to "frame things". If a difficulty arises, you could view yourself as the victim and blame someone else for it, *or...* you could see it as something that is going to help you learn and grow: an opportunity.

Challenges are an expected part of life, and if you see them as opportunities, they might even become exciting and stimulate your creativity. Think about it: do you learn more when things go smoothly or when you have to get creative to overcome life's hurdles? Tapping into your creativity is a hell of a lot more empowering than falling victim to helplessness or self-deprecation.

Activity

a. With pen and paper at hand, think about a recent difficult situation that you struggled to address.

b. Break it down to the facts: what happened, what are the causes and effects, where do you stand in all this.

c. Clarify to yourself the outcome you want from this situation and write it down in a sentence.

d. Now look at how this situation could actually become a useful challenge for you. Make a list that starts with "Enables me to…" (and fill in the blanks). For example, you may find that addressing a conflict situation might be a great opportunity to *enable* you to improve giving feedback and asking for what you want.

e. Now that you know what the enabling factors are for you, make a list of different things you can do that will lead you to your desired outcome. Skills and capabilities are built over time, so why not start now to practice?

f. How do you feel about your challenge now?

Resources

Frankl, Victor – Man's Search for Meaning

Gasca, Leticia – Don't Fail Fast - Fail Mindfully

99. Know that, 'this too shall pass'

"For our light and momentary troubles are achieving for us an eternal glory that far outweighs them all. ***18*** *So we fix our eyes not on what is seen, but on what is unseen, since what is seen is temporary, but what is unseen is eternal." 2 Carinthians 17-18*

In the best of times and in the worst of times, `this too shall pass'.

Iyanla Vanzant, prolific author focusing on spirituality once said, we can make it on broken pieces. Meaning the human spirit has a huge capacity for seeing things through and getting to the other side, no matter the situation.

Viktor Frankl, Neurologist, Psychiatrist and Holocaust survivor also talks about this when he says we can choose our attitude, moment to moment, in any given situation. He cites this as one of our last human freedoms. We have an ability, he says, to either change the situation or change our attitude towards that situation. The consideration of this feels hard sometimes, particularly if you really don't like the options. This is where your resilience kicks in: the ability to choose the best available option or to create a path that you hadn't thought of before.

Activity

a. Identify an issue you have been grappling with.

b. Brainstorm every possible solution you can think of. Do this without second-guessing yourself or judging the options. The point here is to get down on paper as many solutions as possible and only after that make decisions about the way forward.

c. A variant on b. above: Ask a friend to write down all the options you come up with as they come to you. This way, you free yourself from having to do the thinking and writing at the same time, and only concentrate on the thinking and throwing out your ideas.

Resources

Salzgeber, Jonas – The Little Book Of Stoicism

Goggins, David – The Most Eye Opening 10 Minutes Of Your Life

100. Reframe some of the most negative words or phrases you tell yourself

"Our key to transforming anything lies in our ability to reframe it." Marianne Williamson

"To frame or express (words, or a concept or plan) differently" (online dictionary).

"Reframing is when an undesirable behaviour or trait is conferred a positive intention. Alternatives to satisfy the positive intent are found…." NLP World (NLP - Neuro-linguistic Programming. It is a practice of understanding how people communicate).

When considering reframing some of the negative things you might tell yourself, the following questions will be helpful:

In what ways could I turn this negative thought into a positive?

What did I do well?

What aspect of this didn't go so well that I could learn from?

What aspects of this situation *went* well that I can continue to learn from?

Examples of negative words that you could reframe to positive are as follows:

Compulsive → liking detail/paying attention to detail

Self-obsessed → confident in own beliefs and values

Over-bearing → assertive

Got a lot to say for yourself → expressive

Activity

a. Have a notebook with you and on a daily basis, as soon as you notice your negative self-talk, write down the words that you are saying to yourself.

b. Scan the above on a daily/weekly basis and replace each of the phrases with more empowering words and phrases and start telling yourself these words and phrases instead.

c. Write down the changes that you notice about yourself from undertaking b. above.

d. Be warrior-like in your determination to reframe the words and phrases that don't serve you.

Resources

Virtue, Doreen – Don't Let Anything Dull Your Sparkle: How To Break Free Of Negativity And Drama

Connor, Jessica – Five Minute Mind Exercise

101. Visualise a successful outcome

"When you visualize, then you materialize." *Denis Waitley*

When you want to be successful in a feat, a great technique to use is visualising that success in advance. Think about athletes before a competition. They put regular effort in preparing for the race. They prepare physically, of course, and they also prepare mentally.

Mental preparation often involves visualising in your head the trajectory, obstacles and ways to overcome those obstacles, *before* the actual race. Swimmers, climbers and other sports people often use mental visualisation to prepare their strategy, and also to boost their confidence. By seeing themselves as victorious, they increase their chances of succeeding.

Activity

a. Pen and paper at hand, think about a slightly scary project or feat that you are about to undertake. Write it down in a short sentence. For example, you might be doing a presentation in front of 50 people next month.

b. Visualise the environment in detail, as if you were watching a movie. Write down all the details about the people involved, the material and things around you, the place and what it looks like – including space and setup.

c. Now visualise yourself preparing for it before going in: how do you feel beforehand? What are you doing 30 minutes, 10 minutes and 1 minute before going in to deliver the presentation?

c. Now you're in and you're being very successful. Visualise and write down what you're thinking, feeling and doing while you're delivering the presentation in the way you want, from beginning to end. Be detailed about your body language: what it looks like, what it feels like and what it is communicating to the audience. Write about the audience reactions – as you see them happening. Visualise what you are saying in your presentation that is getting the audience engaged. Write about your thought process and how you're handling any difficult questions. Are you smiling? Are you involving the audience? What is it that you're doing that is making it interesting? When you feel like you've gone through it, write down how you will end the presentation in a memorable way, and how you will exit.

d. Reflect on what you have written: has it given you any ideas? What have you noticed? What are you going to learn or practice so that you can get yourself there on the day? What are you going to ask for to set it up the way you want it to be? Anything else?

Resources

Canfield, Jack – The Success Principles: How to Get from Where You Are to Where You Want to Be

Athlete Equanimity – How to Visualize like a Pro

102. Recognise your circle of influence

"We are not a product of what has happened to us in our past. We have the power of choice." Stephen Covey

Take a piece of paper and draw two circles, one inside the other. The inner circle is called the circle of Influence, the outer circle is the circle of Concern. The circle of influence represents what you can control in any given situation. The circle of concern represents what you can't control.

It is common to worry about things that are outside of your area of control, be it the weather, political turmoil, someone else's behaviour or the overall outcome of a project. However, worrying about what is out of your control is draining and ineffective, and it literally shrinks your circle of influence. This in turn affects your feelings, making you feel like you have no power or agency in the situation.

Flip it around and, you've guessed, if you focus more on what you can do, your circle of influence expands, and so does your feeling of agency and empowerment in a given situation. This is because you are consciously focusing your attention and energy on what you *can* do, and there is usually *something* you can do. There are always choices you can make; however small they may be. Resilient people choose where to focus their attention where it most serves them. Are you with me? Let's practice.

Activity

a. Think about a difficult situation you are currently going through (work or otherwise).

b. Draw the inner and outer circle in a way that represents your feeling of agency at the moment (if you feel empowered, your inner circle will be big, otherwise it will be small).

c. Think about where you tend to put your attention. Think about where you want to focus your attention.

d. Populate the outer circle with words that describe concerns, worries, events, behaviours – anything that you can't control in this situation.

e. Populate the inner circle with words that describe what you can do or control in this situation. Does this help you see better what you *can* control?

Resources

Covey, Stephen – The Seven Habits of Highly Effective People

Franklin Covey – Circle of Influence

103. Decide how you are going to view a situation

"The 3C's in Life" Choice, Chance, Change. You must make the choice, to take the chance, if you want anything in life to change." Zig Ziglar

Some situations are difficult to deal with and we can see them in that way. 'This is hard'. 'I don't know what to do'. 'This sucks'. 'I can't see a way out'. Just know, this is a mindset. A way of seeing a situation.

We could just as easily see the same situation in an opposing way. 'There is a solution here'. 'This might be hard for right now, I know though, there is a way around, under, over or through it'. Moment to moment, we have an opportunity to decide our choices and take a chance to make a change. Not wanting to sound glib because there are times in different situations, in different parts of the world where people can't see or experience choices. I would just ask, in whatever situation you find yourself in, ask yourself this question: 'How am I going to view this situation and is there anything I can do to change it?'

Activity

a. Think about a time in your life when you experienced a situation that seemed so monumental, you just didn't know how to tackle it and yet you did the best you could in the situation.

b. With the benefit of hindsight, take a look at that situation again. Consider how you would deal with the situation now, with the benefit of more life experience. What would you do differently and why?

c. Your answer to b. above lays some important life lessons you can incorporate into your own life and pass on to others. Note down your lessons learned and how these have helped you in your life.

Resources

Dyer, Wayne W – Change Your Thoughts Change Your Life: Living the Wisdom of the Tao

Washington, Denzel – Dream Big: Change Your Life

104. Look for opportunities inside the difficulties

"If a window of opportunity appears, don't pull down the shade." Tom Peters

Understanding that difficult situations also create opportunities is key to our wellbeing. In the most problematic circumstances people find a way to 'thrive', or at least transcend, their circumstances. Oprah Winfrey, Terry Waite, Victor Frankl and Iyana Vanzant for example transcended their circumstances to be who they are. It doesn't mean it's easy, it just means it's possible.

Toni Morrison once said: 'If you want to fly, you have to give up the things that weigh you down'.

Activity

a. Look at the potential opportunities you have in front of you (or those you might create).

b. Consider how you might take advantage of these.

c. Think about what you might need to give up, in order to stop being weighed down.

Resources

Reid, Melanie – The World I Fell Out Of

Cantwell, Marianne – The Hidden Power Of Not Always Fitting In

105. Use catastrophising as a creative technique

"The mind is its own place and can make a heaven of hell and a hell of heaven." John Milton

Having catastrophic thoughts can be very unsettling and even depressing, however it doesn't necessarily have to make your worries sky-rocket. Instead, it can be a very creative way to prepare for the worst.

If you're prepared for the worst possible scenario, nothing from here to there will phase you. In addition, by breaking down the worst-case scenario, you will be able to distinguish between what is realistic and what is "fantasy", or just a product of your worry-monster. Being realistic is what will help you prepare effectively for what may come, and everything in between.

Activity

a. Think about an upcoming situation that is worrying you or stressing you out, because you are afraid there might be a terrible outcome.

b. Pen and paper at hand, write down what the worst-case scenario might look like. Be realistic about it, though. Don't include earthquakes and the likes! If you are running a presentation, your worst case scenario could include things like: when you arrive, the IT system isn't working so you can't use slides; the audience includes some subject matter experts who are likely to ask very specific questions; there is a difficult delegate who is constantly on their phone; and you forget one of the key messages you wanted to say.

c. Now that you have broken this down to a realistic worst-case scenario, it probably doesn't look as bad as before. You can manage these aspects one by one if you prepare for them in advance. Take a look at each difficulty one by one, and note down all the things you can do to overcome each hurdle and how you're going to do them, both beforehand and in the moment. For example, what is your plan B if the IT doesn't work? You might plan for handouts in advance, or make sure you don't rely completely on slides (in which case, note down how you're going to do that). If you think you might forget some key points, what are you going to do that will help you remember them? Perhaps you might prepare something on the flipchart before you start, so you are sure you will have the key points at hand. Go through each hurdle and write down in detail all the ways you will handle it if it comes to happen.

d. How are you feeling now? If you are prepared for a realistic worst-case scenario, nothing in between will phase you!

Resources

Judkins, Rod – The Art of Creative Thinking

Corazza, Giovanni – Creative thinking - how to get out of the box and generate ideas

106. Put things into perspective

"If your heart is broken, make art with the pieces." Shane Koyczan

Ever felt like a problem got out of hand and became this huge thing you couldn't stop thinking about? Perhaps it is something that has already happened and you're mulling over it, or it is something that is yet to happen, and you're imagining all the different ways it could go wrong.

Worrying often leads to perceiving an issue as bigger than it actually is. This is also influenced by what else is going on in your life and your perceived ability to cope with it all. Sometimes what you can do is put it into perspective. This doesn't mean discounting the issue, but seeing it more clearly in the grand scheme of things. Make sense?

Activity

a. Pick an issue that has been bothering you, that you would like to put into perspective.

b. Write down your feelings about it, and what you worry might happen.

c. Stop and breathe. Close your eyes. Imagine you are floating toward the sky and you look back down at yourself and your situation as a whole. Now you are floating further out toward the atmosphere, seeing everything else that is around you: all the other people, the environment, how everything is interconnected. You have reached space and you are looking at the Earth. You can now hardly see all the people in the world who are going about their lives. What now catches your eye are the mountains and the oceans. Everything seems slower and more peaceful. The sense of importance of things has shifted, in the grand scheme of things. How are you feeling now, floating above it all? As you keep on breathing, slowly bring yourself back.

d. Note down your thoughts and realisations from the visualisation. Has your way of thinking of the problem shifted? In what way?

e. Is there anything else you can do to deal with this issue?

f. When similar issues arise in the future, what might help you address them?

Resources

Hillenbrand, Laura – Unbroken

ReachINReachOUT – Putting It into Perspective

107. Write yourself a letter from the future

"Life is a succession of lessons which must be lived to be understood." Ralph Waldo Emerson

Growing up and overcoming hurdles makes us older….and wiser! Wouldn't it be great to have a peek into the future and know what lies ahead. Or perhaps it could be even more interesting to get a peek into your own wisdom.

While the crystal ball hasn't been invented yet – perhaps for the best! – it is a wonderful creative exercise to imagine yourself living in the future and to give yourself some insights – perhaps even some advice – from the future. After all, you are your own best advisor. Try it out and have fun! There might be some surprises.

Activity

a. Set aside 30 minutes for yourself and find a quiet spot where you can sit with pen and letter paper, without any distraction. If you need more time, take all the time you need!

b. Close your eyes and imagine yourself in the future. Pick a date in the future: 10, 20, even 30 years from now. Imagine you have 'tele transported' yourself to that time.

c. Start writing to your younger self from that time, knowing that you can post your letter into the past and that your younger self will receive it in their time dimension.

d. What message do you want to give to your younger self? What piece of advice would offer to help your younger self face the challenges that are to come?

e. Anything else that comes to mind?

f. Enclose the letter in an envelope and seal it. Write your name and address on the envelope and either place it somewhere in the house, or post it to yourself through the mail. Wait one week before you open it.

g. You are now back in your younger self, and you "receive" your letter-from-the-future. Open the letter and read it now. Does it offer any insights? Note down your present thoughts.

Resources

Kishime, Ichiro & Koga, Fumitake – The Courage To Be Disliked: How to free yourself, change your life and achieve real happiness

David, Susan – How to Be Your Best Self in Times of Crisis

About the Authors

Hyacinth Fraser

Hyacinth Fraser is a charismatic, action-focused, strategically minded Management Consultant and Trainer. Bouncing Back has been a labour of love precipitated by the unprecedented COVID-19 times. During her thirty years' career, Hyacinth has supported thousands of people to discover their full potential. She is passionate about helping people with their personal growth, self-development and professional success.

You can find more information about Hyacinth on https://uk.linkedin.com/in/hyacinthfraser

Eva Provedel

Eva Provedel is a Leadership Coach, Communication Trainer and Laughter Yoga Teacher who helps professionals develop the skills and confidence to lead from a place of empowerment and happiness. Eva speaks six languages and has lived in three continents. She is passionate about helping others grow and develop. In her spare time, she loves to dance tango and travel the world to explore different cultures and cuisines. You can find more information about Eva's work on www.linkedin.com/in/evaprovedel/.

Printed in Poland
by Amazon Fulfillment
Poland Sp. z o.o., Wrocław

62642690R00129